꼭! 잡은 중학 영문법

# GRAMMAR
# CATCH

Book **2**

Happy House

KB037790

# How to Use This Book

## 주요 문법 설명

내신 성적 향상을 위한 필수 영문법을 체계적으로 설명해 줍니다. 여러분이 보다 쉽게 이해할 수 있도록 학교 시험에 자주 출제되는 예문들을 담았습니다.

## Grammar Check-Up

'내신 족집게 문제'를 풀기 위한 워밍업 단계로, 각 단원의 주요 문법에 관한 다양한 문제 풀이를 통해 기초 실력을 확인할 수 있습니다. 우리말 해석 및 영작 문제를 풀며 독해와 작문 실력을 향상시키며, Word Tip을 통해 문제 해결 능력을 키울 수 있습니다.

## 내신 족집게 문제

각 단원의 문법 사항 중에서 학교 시험에 자주 출제되는 주요 문법 문제들을 엄선하여 주관식과 객관식 문제로 구성했습니다. 문법 문제를 보다 쉽게 풀 수 있는 노하우를 알려드립니다.

## 수능 감각 기르기

사고력과 분석력을 키워 주는 문제들을 통해 중학교 영문법에 자신감을
갖게 됩니다. 앞서 학습한 단계의 문제들을 기반으로 수능 문제에 대한
감각을 키울 수 있도록 구성했습니다.

## 서술형 즐기기

그림이나 표를 이용한 서술형 문제를 다양하게 접할 수 있습니다.
앞서 학습한 Grammar Check-Up의 영작 문제에서 확장된
'한 단락 영작 학습'을 통해 Writing 실력을 향상시킬 수 있습니다.

## Workbook

본책에서 학습한 내용을 복습하고 각 Unit 별로
더욱 다양한 유형의 문제들을 풀어 보면서 배운 문법을
완벽히 마스터할 수 있도록 도와줍니다.

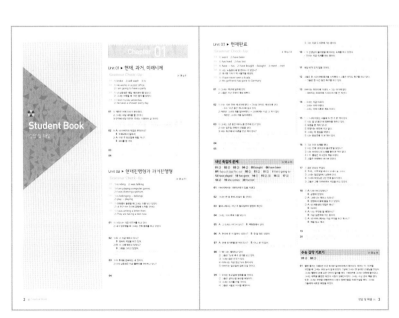

## 정답 및 해설

본책 및 워크북에서 여러분이 푼 문제들에 대한 정답과 저자의
명쾌한 해설이 담겨 있습니다. 문제를 풀면서 미처 생각하지
못하고 넘어간 부분을 확인하고, 틀린 문제는 다시 한 번 풀어 보세요.

# Contents

# Chapter

## 01

시제

### Chapter 미리보기

| 현재시제 | 동사의 현재형 | He plays the piano every day. |
|---|---|---|
| 과거시제 | 동사의 과거형 | He played the piano. |
| 미래시제 | will (= be going to) + 동사원형 | He will play the piano. |
| 현재진행형 | am/are/is + 동사원형-ing | He is playing the piano. |
| 과거진행형 | was/were + 동사원형-ing | He was playing the piano. |
| 현재완료 | have/has + 과거분사(p.p) | He has played the piano. |

Practice makes perfect
▶ 연습은 완벽을 만든다.

# Unit 01 현재, 과거, 미래시제

**Tips**
• 시제란 시간의 흐름을 동사로 표현한 것을 말한다. 영어에서는 총 12개의 시제가 있다.

| 현재시제 | 동사의 현재형 | He plays the piano every day. |
|---|---|---|
| 과거시제 | 동사의 과거형 | He played the piano. |
| 미래시제 | will (= be going to) + 동사원형 | He will play the piano. |

## A 현재시제

**Tips**
• 현재의 반복적인 동작이나 습관은 보통 빈도부사(always, usually, often, sometimes, never 등)와 함께 잘 쓰인다.

현재의 반복적 동작이나 상태, 습관, 속담, 불변의 진리, 일반적·과학적 사실 등을 나타낸다.

**ex** • I always drink coffee without sugar. (반복적 동작)
   • The walls have ears. (속담)
   • Five times five makes twenty five. (일반적 사실)

## B 과거시제

과거의 동작이나 상태, 역사적 사실 등을 나타낸다.
주로 과거를 나타내는 부사구(yesterday, last, ago 등)와 함께 쓴다.

**ex** • He died last year.
   • Japan attacked the American navy in Hawaii in 1940.

## C 미래시제

미래에 일어날 동작이나 상태 등을 나타내며, 조동사 will이나 be going to를 사용한다.

**ex** • She will be a model.
   • They are going to learn Chinese.

⊕ 시간을 나타내는 접속사(when, until, before 등)와 조건을 나타내는 접속사(if)가 이끄는 문장에서는 현재시제가 미래시제를 대신한다.

**ex** • If it snows tomorrow, we will have a snowball fight. (○)
   • If it will snow tomorrow, we will have a snowball fight. (×)

○1 주어진 말을 알맞은 형태로 바꾸어 빈칸에 쓰시오.

1) Karen _____ her leg yesterday. (break)

2) She _____ her car tomorrow. (wash)

3) If it _____ hot tomorrow, we will go swimming. (be)

○2 주어진 말을 이용하여 질문에 대한 대답을 쓰시오.

1) Ⓐ What does your father do?

Ⓑ _____

(work in a post office)

2) Ⓐ What are you going to do this Saturday?

Ⓑ _____

(have a party)

2) have a party
파티를 열다

○3 다음 문장을 우리말로 해석하시오.

1) My brother reads *Harry Potter* books every day.

→ _____

2) She read *The Little Prince* when she was young.

→ _____

○4 다음 우리말을 영작하시오.

1) 나는 어제 열쇠를 잃어버렸다.

→ _____

2) 그는 매일 샤워를 한다.

→ _____

1) lose (– lost – lost)
잃어버리다

2) take a shower
샤워하다

# Unit 02 현재진행형과 과거진행형

| 현재진행형 | am/are/is + 동사원형-ing | (지금) ~하는 중이다, ~하고 있다 |
|---|---|---|
| 과거진행형 | was/were + 동사원형-ing | (과거) ~하는 중이었다, ~하고 있었다 |

## A 현재진행형

현재 하고 있는 동작을 나타낸다.

ex
- A: What are you doing now?
  B: I am talking to my sister.
- Listen! She is playing the flute.

## B 과거진행형

과거의 어느 한 순간 하고 있었던 동작을 나타낸다.

ex
- A: What were you doing then?
  B: I was having a chat with my friend.
- I was talking on the phone when you called me.

## C 진행형에서 주의사항

1 현재진행형은 미래를 나타내는 부사구(soon, tomorrow, next 등)와 함께 쓰여, 가까운 미래를 나타낼 수 있다.

ex
- My father is coming back tonight. (아버지께서는 오늘 밤 돌아오실 것이다.)
- The bus for Busan is leaving soon. (부산행 버스가 곧 출발할 것이다.)

2 소유(have, belong to 등), 감정(like, love, want 등), 감각(see, hear, taste 등), 인지(know 등)를 나타내는 동사들은 진행형과 같이 쓸 수 없다. 하지만, 동작을 나타내는 의미로 쓰일 때는 진행형을 쓸 수 있다.

ex
- He has a lot of books. (○)
- He is having a lot of books. (×)
- He is having lunch. (○)
- Kimchi tastes hot. (○)
- Kimchi is tasting hot. (×)
- My mother is tasting the kimchi. (○)

○1 **주어진 말을 알맞은 형태로 바꾸어 빈칸에 쓰시오.**

1) Chris _____ _____ a bicycle now. (ride)

2) She _____ _____ on the phone when I visited her. (talk)

○2 **주어진 말을 이용하여 질문에 대한 대답을 쓰시오.**

1) Ⓐ What are you doing now?

　Ⓑ _____

　　　　　　　　(play computer games)

2) Ⓐ What were you doing then?

　Ⓑ _____

　　　　　　　　(draw a picture)

○3 **다음 문장의 틀린 부분에 밑줄을 긋고 바르게 고쳐 쓰시오.**

1) This laptop computer is belonging to me.　　(→ _____ )

2) Is your brother play the flute now?　　(→ _____ )

1) laptop computer 휴대용 컴퓨터

○4 **다음 문장을 우리말로 해석하시오.**

1) She was brushing her teeth when the phone rang.

　→ _____

2) My friend, Sue, is arriving at the airport at 5 o'clock.

　→ _____

1) ring (– rang – rung) (전화가) 울리다

2) arrive at ~에 도착하다

○5 **다음 우리말을 영작하시오.**

1) 나는 그때 편지를 쓰던 중이었다.

　→ _____

2) 그들은 지금 시험을 치르는 중이다.

　→ _____

1) write a letter 편지를 쓰다

2) take a test 시험을 치르다

## A 현재완료의 의미

현재완료는 〈have + 과거분사(p.p)〉의 형태이며, 과거의 한 시점부터 현재까지의 기간에 걸친 경험, 계속, 완료, 결과 등을 나타낸다.

> **ex** • She moved to Seoul two years ago. (과거) + She still lives in Seoul. (현재)
>   → She has lived in Seoul for two years. (현재완료)

## B 현재완료와 과거시제

| 과거시제 | 현재완료 |
|---|---|
| • 과거만을 표현<br>I was sick yesterday. | • 과거와 현재를 같이 표현<br>I have been sick since yesterday. |
| • 의문사 when, 과거를 나타내는 부사구와 함께 사용할 수 있다.<br>When did you buy the book? (○)<br>I met her last night. (○) | • 의문사 when, 과거를 나타내는 부사구와 함께 사용할 수 없다.<br>When have you bought the book? (×)<br>I have met her last night. (×) |

## C 현재완료의 용법

1 **경험** : 과거부터 현재까지의 경험을 표현하며, '~한 적이 있다(없다)'로 해석한다.
   주로 ever, never, once, twice 등과 함께 쓰인다.

> **ex** • A: Have you ever heard any of the Beatles' songs?
>    B: Yes, I have.

2 **계속** : 과거부터 현재까지 계속 해 오고 있는 것을 표현하며, '계속 ~해 오고 있다'로 해석한다.
   주로 for, since 등과 함께 쓰인다.

> **ex** • My father has talked to us for two hours.
>   • She has been busy since last week.

3 **완료** : 과거부터 해 온 일을 방금 끝냈다는 표현이며, '막 ~했다'로 해석한다.
   주로 just, already, yet 등과 함께 쓰인다.

> **ex** • Karen has just eaten lunch.
>   • He has not finished the work yet.

4 **결과** : 과거에 일어난 일이 현재에 영향을 미치는 것을 표현하며, '~해서 …하다'로 해석한다.

> **ex** • My friend has gone to Hungary. (내 친구는 헝가리에 가고 지금 여기에 없다.)

# Grammar Check-Up

**O1** 다음 중 알맞은 것을 고르시오.

1) She   has gone ∣ went   to Japan last year.

2) They   were ∣ have been   busy since last week.


**O2** 다음 두 문장을 한 문장으로 나타낼 때 빈칸에 들어갈 알맞은 말을 쓰시오.

1) Sue came to Canada ten years ago. + She still lives in Canada.

　→ Sue _____ _____ in Canada for ten years.

2) Karen lost her dog. + She doesn't have it now.

　→ Karen _____ _____ her dog.


**O3** 다음 문장의 틀린 부분에 밑줄을 긋고 바르게 고쳐 쓰시오.

1) He have played the piano for two years.　(→ _____ )

2) I have bought these shoes a week ago.　(→ _____ )

3) Have you meet your cousin lately?　(→ _____ )

3) lately 최근에


**O4** 다음 문장을 우리말로 해석하시오.

1) How many times have you been to New Zealand?

　→ _____

2) The train for Daegu has just left Seoul Station.

　→ _____

2) leave (– left – left) 떠나다


**O5** 다음 우리말을 영작하시오.

1) 나는 코알라(koala)를 본 적이 없다.

　→ _____

2) 그의 여자 친구는 독일로 가버리고 없다.

　→ _____

# 내신 족집게 문제

**[01-04] 빈칸에 들어갈 알맞은 것을 고르시오.**

**01** My father _____ this house in 1985.

① buy      ② will buy      ③ bought
④ is buying      ⑤ has bought

**02** She _____ twenty years old in a month.

① is      ② was      ③ has been
④ have been      ⑤ will be

**03** My grandmother _____ in the hospital since last Monday.

① is      ② was      ③ has been
④ have been      ⑤ will be

**04** She _____ her teeth after she eats every meal.

① brush      ② brushes      ③ brushed
④ is brushing      ⑤ has brushed

**[05-07] 대화의 빈칸에 알맞은 말을 쓰시오.**

**05** A: Where did you buy the dress?

B: I _____ it at the department store.

**06** A: How long have you been in Korea?

B: I _____ _____ in Korea for a month.

**07** A: Have you ever seen a kangaroo before?

B: No, _____ _____.

**08** 다음 중 어법상 틀린 문장을 고르시오.

① Look! He is washing his car.
② They are watching a soccer game on TV.
③ She is having a lot of friends.
④ My mother is having lunch now.
⑤ My father is coming back home on Sunday.

**09** 밑줄 친 부분의 의미가 나머지와 다른 것을 고르시오.

① We are going to see a movie on Saturday.
② They are going to climb Mt. Seorak.
③ She is going to make pizza.
④ They are going to move to Seoul.
⑤ He is going to the library now.

**10** 빈칸에 알맞은 단어를 순서대로 바르게 짝지은 것을 고르시오.

• When the teacher came in, we _____ our homework.
• We _____ our homework now.

① are doing – were doing
② are doing – are doing
③ were doing – are doing
④ were doing – were doing
⑤ were doing – doing

**11** 두 문장의 뜻이 같도록 빈칸에 알맞은 말을 쓰시오.

It won't rain tomorrow.

= It _____ _____ _____ rain tomorrow.

[12-13] 다음 두 문장을 한 문장으로 나타낼 때 빈칸에 들어갈 알맞은 말을 쓰시오.

12  They started to play soccer an hour ago. + They are still playing soccer.

→ They _____ _____ soccer for an hour.

13  My dad went to Hawaii. + He is not here.

→ My dad _____ _____ to Hawaii.

14  빈칸에 알맞은 단어를 순서대로 바르게 짝지은 것을 고르시오.

· She _____ sick now.
· She _____ sick yesterday.
· She _____ sick since yesterday.

① is – was – has been    ② is – was – was
③ is – has been – was    ④ was – was – was
⑤ has been – has been – was

15  보기의 밑줄 친 부분과 용법이 같은 것을 두 개 고르시오.

보기  My aunt has been to Seoul twice.

① I have wanted a new computer for a year.
② Have you ever seen a ghost?
③ Minyeong has gone to Daejeon.
④ She has just eaten lunch.
⑤ I have been to the broadcasting station.

16  다음 중 어법상 틀린 문장을 고르시오.

① He has already done his homework.
② When have you read *Romeo and Juliet*?
③ I have never heard Britney's songs.
④ J. K. Rowling has just finished 6 books.
⑤ They have been here since yesterday.

17  밑줄 친 부분이 어법상 틀린 것을 고르시오.

① Gold is heavier than silver.
② We will play outside until it will get dark.
③ She goes to church every Sunday.
④ Her parents died two years ago.
⑤ They were playing the game of rock-paper-scissors then.

18  다음 중 대화가 어색한 것을 고르시오.

① Ⓐ Where have you been?
  Ⓑ I have been to the airport.
② Ⓐ What were you doing at that time?
  Ⓑ I was watering flowers in the garden.
③ Ⓐ What does your sister do?
  Ⓑ She is a doctor.
④ Ⓐ What are you going to do?
  Ⓑ I am going to my uncle's house now.
⑤ Ⓐ What is your mother doing now?
  Ⓑ She is reading books.

[19-20] 우리말과 일치하도록 빈칸에 알맞은 말을 쓰시오.

19  만약 그녀가 내일 돌아오면, 나는 그녀를 용서할 것이다.

→ If _____ _____ back tomorrow, I will forgive her.

20  나는 버스에서 지갑을 잃어버려서 돈이 하나도 없다.

→ _____ _____ my wallet on the bus, so I have no money.

O1 다음 글의 밑줄 친 부분 중 어법상 **틀린** 것을 고르시오.

> In 1880, Helen Keller ① was born in northwest Alabama, USA. When she was nineteen months old, she became deaf and blind. ② At the age of seven, she met a teacher, Miss Ann Sullivan. She spelled all the words in Helen's hand. In 1900, she ③ went to college. She was the first deaf and blind person to graduate from college. She ④ has written dozens of books. Also, as she traveled all over the country, she gave speeches about the deaf and blind. She ⑤ gave new hope to them.

- spell 철자를 쓰다    - graduate 졸업하다
- the deaf and blind 시청각 장애인들

O2 다음 빈칸에 들어갈 말로 가장 적절한 것을 고르시오.

> Sue and Tim Ⓐ_____ married in 2005. They Ⓑ_____ married for 10 years. Today is their 10th wedding anniversary. They wanted to celebrate it with their friends, so they sent invitation cards to them. Sue and Tim prepared for the party all day long. Many friends came to the house and had a good time. However, Sue and Tim were too tired to enjoy the party.

- 10th wedding anniversary 결혼 10주년
- celebrate 축하하다

|  | Ⓐ |  | Ⓑ |
|---|---|---|---|
| ① | get | – | have been |
| ② | got | – | were |
| ③ | got | – | have been |
| ④ | have got | – | were |
| ⑤ | have got | – | have been |

O1 자연스러운 대화가 되도록 주어진 단어를 이용하여 빈칸에 알맞은 말을 쓰시오.

Ⓐ Where were you at 6 p.m. yesterday?

Ⓑ _____
　　　　　　　　　(at home)

Ⓐ What were you doing at home then?

Ⓑ _____
　　　　　　　　　(watch TV)

Ⓐ What did you watch on TV?

Ⓑ _____
　　　　　　　(Solomon's Choice)

Ⓐ You are lying. *Solomon's Choice* wasn't on at that time.

O2 다음 우리말을 읽고 바르게 영작하시오.

민영 : 너 지금 뭐하고 있니?
인태 : 내 자동차 열쇠를 찾고 있어.
　　　 찾을 수가 없네. 잃어버렸어.
민영 : 차 안을 찾아 보자.
인태 : 뭐라고?

Minyeong : _____

Intae 　　 : _____

_____

Minyeong : Let's look for it in the car.

Intae 　　 : What?

# Chapter 02

조동사

## Chapter 미리보기

| 가능, 능력 | can | | ~할 수 있다 | | 추측 | may | ~일지도 모른다 |
|---|---|---|---|---|---|---|---|
| 허락 | can, may | | ~해도 좋다 | | | must | ~임에 틀림없다 |
| 의무 | must, have to (강한 의무) | | ~해야만 한다 | | | cannot (= can't) | ~일 리가 없다 |
| | should (도덕적 의무) | | | | 요청, 부탁 | can, could, will, would | ~해 주시겠습니까? |

▶ 물에 빠진 사람은 지푸라기라도 잡는다.

# 04 can, may, will

## A can

### 1 능력 (~할 수 있다)

**ex** • I can (= am able to) speak English.
   • He could (= was able to) play the violin.
   • She will be able to come.

### 2 허락 (~해도 좋다)

**ex** • Can I borrow your book?

### 3 추측 (~일 수도 있다)

**ex** • Studying can be fun.
   • He cannot (= can't) be an English teacher. (부정 : ~일 리 없다)

### 4 요청 (~해 주시겠습니까?)

**ex** • Can (= Could) you carry it for me, please?

## B may

### 1 약한 추측 (~일지도 모른다)

**ex** • She may be right.

### 2 허락 (~해도 좋다)

**ex** • You may go now.

## C will

### 1 미래, 의지 (~할 것이다)

**ex** • I will (= am going to) meet my friend.
   • I will keep my promise.
   • I won't go to the movies.

### 2 요청, 권유, 부탁 (~해 주시겠습니까?, ~하시겠습니까?)

**ex** • Will (= Would) you open the door, please?
   • Would you like to go to the movies?
   • Would you like some milk?

# Grammar Check-Up

정답 및 해설 p.4

**O1** 다음 중 알맞은 것을 고르시오.

1) We  can ┃ will can  dance ballet here.

2) Would you  like to ┃ like  some apple juice?

**O2** 두 문장의 뜻이 같도록 빈칸에 알맞은 말을 쓰시오.

1) He can play the flute.

= He _____ _____ _____ play the flute.

2) She wants to explore the North Pole.

= She _____ _____ _____ explore the North Pole.

3) It will rain.

= It _____ _____ _____ rain.

2) explore  탐험하다
the North Pole  북극

**O3** 다음 문장을 우리말로 해석하시오.

1) I may invite her to my birthday party.

→ _____

2) May I go home?

→ _____

3) John can't be a pilot.

→ _____

3) pilot  조종사

**O4** 우리말과 일치하도록 빈칸에 알맞은 말을 쓰시오.

1) 나는 너와 말하지 않을 것이다.

→ I _____ _____ to you.

2) 나는 다시 시작할 것이다.

→ I _____ _____ again.

3) 나와 함께 소풍 갈래요?

→ _____ you _____ _____ go on a picnic with me?

# 05 must, have to, should, had better

## A must, have to

### 1 의무 (~해야 한다)

ex ▶ • We must (= have to) go to school today.
  • He had to study hard.
  • He will have to do it.
  • A: Must I leave?
    B: Yes, you must. / No, you don't have to.

### 2 강한 추측 (~임에 틀림없다)

ex ▶ • She must be a dentist.

### 3 부정문

| | | |
|---|---|---|
| 의무 | don't have to = don't need to (~할 필요 없다) | We don't have to do our homework today. |
| | must not (~하면 안 된다) | They must not open the box. |
| 추측 | cannot (= can't) (~일 리 없다) | It can't be true. |

## B should

의무: ~해야 한다

ex ▶ • You should keep your promises.
  • You should not tell a lie.

## C had better

충고: ~하는 것이 좋다

ex ▶ • You had better stay here.
  • You'd better tell the truth.
  • You'd better not watch TV all day.

**01** 다음 중 알맞은 것을 고르시오.

1) You   must | must not   touch the painting.

2) We   should | shouldn't   give up our seats to elderly people.

3) You   have | had   better be quiet.

2) give up 양보하다
elderly people
노인들

**02** 다음 문장을 지시대로 바꾸어 쓰시오.

1) She must go to the dentist.

과거시제 ▶ _____

2) You had better do it.

부정문 ▶ _____

1) dentist 치과의사

**03** 다음 문장을 우리말로 해석하시오.

1) Mr. Green must be a politician.

→ _____

2) It is Sunday. I don't have to wake up early.

→ _____

3) Children must not play with matches.

→ _____

1) politician 정치가
3) match 성냥

**04** 우리말과 일치하도록 빈칸에 알맞은 말을 쓰시오.

1) 너는 그것을 다른 사람들에게 말하면 안 된다.

→ You should _____ _____ it to others.

2) 너는 오늘 숙제를 하는 것이 좋겠다.

→ You'd _____ _____ _____
_____ today.

3) 그가 천재일 리 없다.

→ He _____ _____ a genius.

3) genius 천재

[01-02] 빈칸에 공통으로 들어갈 알맞은 말을 쓰시오.

O1
- _____ I use your pen?
- I _____ speak English fluently.

O2
- _____ you close the window, please?
- I _____ like to go to London.

O3 우리말과 일치하도록 빈칸에 알맞은 말을 쓰시오.

나는 방과 후에 숙제를 함께 하기 위해 제인을 만날 것이다.

→ After school, I _____ meet Jane to do our homework together.

[04-05] 대화의 빈칸에 들어갈 알맞은 것을 고르시오.

O4
A: I couldn't sleep last night. I feel sleepy now.
B: You _____ go home and get some sleep.

① won't      ② would
③ should      ④ would like
⑤ have better

O5
A: I think I saw her in the market this morning.
B: That _____ be true. She is in Canada now.

① had better      ② will
③ must      ④ can't
⑤ would like to

[06-07] 빈칸에 들어갈 알맞은 것을 고르시오.

O6
She _____ go to Canada to see her sister.

① has better      ② would like to
③ have to      ④ would like
⑤ had not better

O7
This is a cheap restaurant, so we _____ spend a lot of money.

① doesn't have to      ② don't have to
③ has to      ④ have to
⑤ will

O8 우리말과 일치하도록 빈칸에 알맞은 말을 쓰시오.

제인, 우산 가져가. 오늘 밤에 비 올지도 몰라.
→ Jane, take an umbrella. It _____ rain tonight.

O9 두 문장이 같은 뜻이 되도록 빈칸에 들어갈 알맞은 것을 고르시오.

She doesn't have to be there.
= She _____ be there.

① had better not      ② doesn't need to
③ must not      ④ cannot
⑤ will not

[10-11] 빈칸에 들어갈 수 없는 것을 고르시오.

10
He _____ be a police officer.

① must      ② can      ③ may
④ has to      ⑤ could

**11** We _____ disturb them.

① must not ② should not
③ would like ④ don't have to
⑤ had better not

**[12-13] 우리말과 일치하도록 빈칸에 알맞은 말을 쓰시오.**

**12** 앤은 내일 공항으로 그를 마중 나가야 할 것이다.

→ Ann _____ _____ _____
pick him up from the airport tomorrow.

**13** 너는 그것을 하지 않는 것이 좋겠다.

→ You'd _____ _____ do that.

**14** 빈칸에 들어갈 알맞은 말을 쓰시오.

Paul just ran a marathon. He _____ be tired now.

**15** 다음 중 어법상 틀린 문장을 고르시오.

① She would like meet the writer.
② We don't have to do it.
③ You had better be on time.
④ Would you like some chocolate?
⑤ He must not enter the room.

**16** 문장의 의미가 나머지와 다른 것을 고르시오.

① Would you help me?
② Can you help me?
③ Must you help me?
④ Could you help me?
⑤ Will you help me?

**17** 밑줄 친 부분의 의미가 나머지와 다른 것을 고르시오.

① They may be our teachers.
② You may use my bike.
③ He may speak Chinese.
④ She may be right.
⑤ They may come to the party.

**[18-19] 보기의 밑줄 친 부분과 의미가 다른 것을 고르시오.**

**18** 보기 She can play a lot of musical instruments.

① I can help these children.
② Can I use your cell phone?
③ She can speak English.
④ Can she swim in the sea?
⑤ He can play tennis.

**19** 보기 John must follow the rules.

① I must tell it to you.
② She must take another exam.
③ They must do it now.
④ It must be true.
⑤ He must do his duty.

**20** 두 문장의 뜻이 같지 않은 것을 고르시오.

① She can't play the flute.
= She isn't able to play the flute.
② He won't go to the United States.
= He will not go to the United States.
③ You must be Tom.
= You can't be Tom.
④ I don't have to go to school today.
= I don't need to go to school today.
⑤ We would like to meet the singers.
= We want to meet the singers.

정답 및 해설 p.5

**01** 다음 글의 밑줄 친 부분 중 어법상 틀린 것을 고르시오.

> My father ① used to climb mountains with my grandfather when he was in his teens. He wants to go to the mountains with me. We are planning to climb Mt. Dobong this weekend. We ② would better check the weather forecast. If it is rainy, we ③ won't go climbing. We ④ should wear a pair of mountain-climbing boots. It can be slippery to climb without the boots. After climbing, we will have a delicious meal near the mountain. Then I ⑤ would like to go to a sauna.

- weather forecast 일기 예보   - slippery 미끄러운

**02** 다음 괄호 안에서 어법에 맞는 표현으로 가장 적절한 것을 고르시오.

> Swimming is good for your health. There are some rules to follow before you go into the water. You **A** (must / may) warm up before swimming. You **B** (must / must not) swim just after having a big meal. You shouldn't go too far while you are swimming in the sea. You **C** (must not / don't have to) wear a swimming cap in the sea.

- warm up 준비 운동을 하다   - swimming cap 수영 모자

| | A | | B | | C |
|---|---|---|---|---|---|
| ① | must | – | must | – | must not |
| ② | must | – | must not | – | must not |
| ③ | must | – | must not | – | don't have to |
| ④ | may | – | must | – | don't have to |
| ⑤ | may | – | must not | – | don't have to |

**01** 다음 그림을 보고 must를 사용하여 빈칸에 알맞은 말을 쓰시오.

1) You _____ here.

2) You _____ here.

3) You _____ here.

**02** 다음 우리말을 읽고 빈칸에 알맞은 말을 쓰시오.

우리 가족은 지금 휴가 중이어서 강가에 있는 호텔에 머물고 있다. 우리는 강에서 큰 물고기를 잡고 싶었지만 거기에는 낚시 금지 표지판이 있어서 우리는 거기에서 낚시를 하면 안 된다. 대신에 우리는 다른 레저 활동을 하는 것이 좋겠다.

Our family is on vacation now and we're staying at a hotel by the river. We were hoping to catch some big fish in the river, but there is a _____ _____ sign there, so we _____ _____ fish there. Instead we'd _____ _____ some other leisure activities to do.

# Chapter 03

대명사

## Chapter 미리보기

| it | 비인칭주어 | It is sunny. | 재귀대명사 | 강조용법 | He made the box himself. |
|---|---|---|---|---|---|
| | 가주어 | It is fun to ski. | | 재귀용법 | We enjoyed ourselves. |

| 부정대명사 | one | 앞에 언급한 막연한 사람, 사물을 가리킴 | |
|---|---|---|---|
| | another | 또 다른 하나, 또 하나의 | |
| | one, the other | 🐱 🐱 | 하나, 나머지 하나 |
| | some, others | 🐱🐱🐱🐱 🐱🐱🐱 | 몇몇, 다른 몇몇 |
| | both | ○ ○ | 둘 디 |
| | either | ○ ✕ | 둘 중의 하나 |
| | neither | ✕ ✕ | 둘 다 아니다 |

One man's meat is another man's poison.

▶ 어떤 사람이 좋아하는 것을 다른 사람은 싫어할 수 있다.

# 06 대명사 it, 재귀대명사

## A 대명사 it

**1** 이미 앞에 나온 특정한 명사를 대신한다.

ex • I liked the movie. Did you like it?

**2** 가주어 it으로 쓰인다.

ex • To speak English is not easy.
   → It is not easy to speak English.
   • Playing football is fun.
   → It is fun playing football.

**3** 비인칭주어 it으로 쓰여 요일, 날씨, 시간, 계절, 명암, 거리 등을 나타낸다.

ex • It is Sunday/5 o'clock/dark.

## B 재귀대명사

**1 재귀용법** : 주어와 목적어가 같을 때 재귀대명사가 동사의 목적어나 전치사의 목적어로 사용되며, 생략이 불가능하다.

ex • I hurt myself. (동사의 목적어)
   • I am proud of myself. (전치사의 목적어)

• enjoy oneself 즐거운 시간을 보내다          • teach oneself 독학하다
   • help oneself  마음껏 먹다                    • kill oneself 자살하다

**2 강조용법** : 주어나 목적어를 강조할 때 사용되며, 생략이 가능하다.

ex • My grandfather (himself) built this house.
   • She married my brother (himself).

**3 관용적 표현**

ex • She had lunch by herself.
   • He finished the work for himself.

### Tips
• by oneself
  홀로(= alone)

• for oneself
  혼자 힘으로

# Grammar Check-Up

**01** 다음 중 알맞은 것을 고르시오.

1) This │ It │ is dark outside.

2) They enjoyed │ them │ themselves │ at Lotte World.

3) He killed │ herself │ himself │ last night.

**02** 다음 문장의 틀린 부분에 밑줄을 긋고 바르게 고쳐 쓰시오.

1) This is sunny. (→ _____ )

2) She read the book but I didn't read one. (→ _____ )

3) That is difficult to answer the question. (→ _____ )

**03** 다음 문장을 우리말로 해석하시오.

1) She went to the movies by herself.

→ _____

2) He himself did the work.

→ _____

3) It is not easy to climb Mt. Everest.

→ _____

**04** 우리말과 일치하도록 빈칸에 알맞은 말을 쓰시오.

1) 나는 나 자신이 자랑스럽다.

→ I am proud _____ _____.

2) 그는 혼자 캐나다를 여행했다.

→ He traveled around Canada _____ _____.

3) 마음껏 드세요.

→ _____ _____.

1) be proud of
~을 자랑스럽게 여기다

## A one

앞에 언급한 막연한 사람, 사물을 가리킨다. 소유격은 one's이며, 복수형은 ones이다.

ex • This dress is more expensive than that one.

| it | 특정한 것을 나타냄 | A: Do you have the book? B: Yes, I have it. |
| --- | --- | --- |
| one | 막연한 것을 나타냄 | A: Do you have a book? B: Yes, I have one. |

## B one, the other

'(둘 중) 하나는 ~, 나머지 하나는 …'를 뜻한다.

ex • I have two pets. One is a dog and the other is a cat.

## C some, others

'(여러 개 중) 몇몇은 ~, 다른 몇몇은 …'을 뜻한다.

ex • There are many flowers in the garden. Some are roses and others are lilies.

## D another

'또 다른 하나'를 뜻한다.

ex • I don't like this bag. Please show me another.

## E each, every

each는 '각각, 각자', every는 '모든'을 뜻한다. 둘 다 단수 취급하며, 단수 동사가 온다.

ex • Each of the students has a cell phone.
• Every boy likes playing soccer.

⊕ each other (둘 사이) 서로    ex • They are looking at each other.

one another (셋 이상) 서로    ex • They want to help one another.

## F both, either, neither

| both | 둘 다 | Both of these books are interesting. |
| --- | --- | --- |
| either | 둘 중의 하나 | I don't like either of the twins. |
| neither | 둘 다 아니다 | Neither of us can speak Chinese. |

**Q1** 빈칸에 알맞은 대명사를 보기에서 골라 쓰시오.

보기    one      it      another      the other      some      others

1) I lost my eraser yesterday. I have to buy a new _____.

2) I don't like this hat. Could you show me _____?

3) Some boys like soccer, and _____ like baseball.

4) I have two foreign friends. One is from China and _____ is from America.

**Q2** 우리말과 일치하도록 빈칸에 알맞은 말을 쓰시오.

1) 나의 부모님은 모두 제주도 출신이시다.

→ _____ of my parents _____ from Jejudo.

2) 그들은 둘 다 내 이름을 기억하지 못했다.

→ _____ of them remembered my name.

**Q3** 다음 문장을 우리말로 해석하시오.

1) Every parent worries about their children.

→ _____

2) Can either of you speak French?

→ _____

3) In a baseball game, each team has 9 players.

→ _____

1) worry about
   ~에 대해 걱정하다

**Q4** 다음 우리말을 영작하시오.

1) 어떤 사람들은 커피를 좋아하고 다른 어떤 사람들은 차를 좋아한다.

→ _____

2) 한 마리는 강아지이고 다른 한 마리는 햄스터이다.

→ _____

2) hamster  햄스터

**01** 우리말과 일치하도록 빈칸에 알맞은 말을 쓰시오.

- 그녀는 다쳤다.
  → She hurt _____.
- 그는 자기 자신을 보았다.
  → He looked at _____.

**02** 빈칸에 들어갈 알맞은 것을 고르시오.

There is a bag on the table. Is _____ yours?

① one　　② it　　③ they
④ those　　⑤ these

**03** 빈칸에 알맞은 재귀대명사를 쓰시오.

I told Jane, "Help _____ to the chocolate."

**[04 - 05] 두 문장의 뜻이 같도록 빈칸에 알맞은 말을 쓰시오.**

**04** To learn a foreign language is interesting.
= _____ _____ _____ to learn a foreign language.

**05** We had a good time at your birthday party.
= We _____ _____ at your birthday party.

**06** 빈칸에 공통으로 들어갈 알맞은 말을 쓰시오.

- _____ is about five kilometers from here to my house.
- _____ is seven-thirty now.

**07** 밑줄 친 재귀대명사 중 생략할 수 <u>없는</u> 것을 고르시오.

① She herself likes him.
② He cooked spaghetti himself.
③ We ourselves fixed our bicycles.
④ They look after themselves.
⑤ I myself won the first prize.

**08** 밑줄 친 부분이 어법상 <u>틀린</u> 것을 고르시오.

① She did it herself.
② They themself painted the room.
③ My father went to the park by himself.
④ My sister saw herself in the mirror.
⑤ Her brother made pizza himself.

**[09 - 10] 밑줄 친 부분의 쓰임이 나머지와 <u>다른</u> 것을 고르시오.**

**09** ① It is Saturday.
② It is about ten kilometers from here.
③ It is my favorite painting.
④ It is raining outside.
⑤ It is half past eleven.

**10** ① He wrote the book himself.
② She is taking care of herself.
③ Let me introduce myself.
④ He taught himself.
⑤ I sometimes talk to myself.

**11** 다음 중 올바른 문장을 고르시오.

① This is dark in this room.
② Each books have ten chapters.
③ Every sentences have a verb.
④ Both of them helped each other.
⑤ I lost my bag and bought it.

12 다음 두 문장을 한 문장으로 나타낼 때 빈칸에 들어갈 알맞은 것을 고르시오.

> My sister, Minyeong, left Seoul yesterday. +
> My sister, Seonghui, left Seoul yesterday, too.
> → _____ of my sisters left Seoul yesterday.

① Both      ② Either      ③ Neither

④ It      ⑤ One

13 빈칸에 공통으로 들어갈 알맞은 것을 고르시오.

> • Could I have _____ cup of coffee?
> • I don't like this shirt. Could you show me _____?

① one      ② other      ③ another

④ it      ⑤ some

[14-15] 빈칸에 들어갈 알맞은 말을 쓰시오.

14 There are two flowers in the vase.

_____ is a rose and _____

_____ is a carnation.

15 Some are walking along the river and

_____ are riding bikes.

16 두 대화의 빈칸에 공통으로 들어갈 알맞은 것을 고르시오.

> • A: Do you want coke or juice?
>   B: _____. It doesn't matter.
> • A: I don't like to watch TV.
>   B: I don't like to watch TV, _____.

① Both      ② Either      ③ Neither

④ It      ⑤ One

17 빈칸에 알맞은 단어를 순서대로 바르게 짝지은 것을 고르시오.

> • Every _____ _____ waiting for you.
> • Both of the _____ _____ 14 years old.

① student – is – students – are

② student – is – students – is

③ student – is – student – is

④ students – are – students – are

⑤ students – are – student – are

18 대화의 빈칸에 알맞은 단어를 순서대로 바르게 짝지은 것을 고르시오.

> • A: Did you find your dog?
>   B: Yes, I found _____.
> • A: Do you have a computer?
>   B: No, I don't. But my sister has _____.
> • A: Which shoes are yours?
>   B: The _____ in front of yours.

① one – one – ones      ② one – it – ones

③ it – one – ones      ④ it – one – one

⑤ it – ones – ones

19 두 문장의 뜻이 같도록 빈칸에 알맞은 말을 쓰시오.

> My friend, Sue, goes to church on Sundays.
> = My friend, Sue, goes to church _____
> _____.

20 우리말과 일치하도록 빈칸에 알맞은 말을 쓰시오.

> 나의 부모님은 서울에 살지 않으신다.
> → _____ of my parents lives in Seoul.

정답 및 해설 p.6

O1 다음 글의 밑줄 친 부분 중 어법상 <u>틀린</u> 것을 고르시오.

> Once upon a time, two friends walked through a forest. Suddenly a bear appeared. ① One friend went up a tree. ② Another man knew that there was ③ nothing he could do, so he fell to the ground and didn't move. The bear walked over to the man on the ground and sniffed about his ears. Because the bear thought that he was dead, ④ it walked away. The man in the tree climbed down and asked, "What did the bear say?" His friend answered, "A good friend helps friends who are in danger." Then the man who played dead went away by ⑤ himself.

- suddenly 갑자기　　- appear 나타나다
- sniff 코를 킁킁 거리다, 냄새를 맡다

O1 다음 글을 읽고 재귀대명사를 사용하여 빈칸에 알맞은 말을 쓰시오.

> John built a house. He did it alone. Then he moved into the house. He was satisfied with it. He is talking to his friend, Paul, about the house.

Paul : Wow! This is a nice house!

John : I built it _____ _____.

Paul : You mean you _____ made it?

John : Of course. I am proud of _____.

O2 다음 괄호 안에서 어법에 맞는 표현으로 가장 적절한 것을 고르시오.

> Last summer I visited my uncle. He lives in California. He was very busy so I went to Universal Studios Ⓐ(of myself / by myself). I took a lot of photos there. Then I went to Hollywood. It is the center of the movie-making world. Ⓑ(It / That) was interesting to see the footprints and autographs of the world famous movie stars. I enjoyed Ⓒ(me / myself) there.

- footprint 발자국　　- autograph 서명

| | Ⓐ | | Ⓑ | | Ⓒ |
|---|---|---|---|---|---|
| ① | of myself | – | It | – | me |
| ② | of myself | – | That | – | myself |
| ③ | of myself | – | That | – | me |
| ④ | by myself | – | That | – | myself |
| ⑤ | by myself | – | It | – | myself |

O2 다음 우리말을 읽고 바르게 영작하시오.

나는 어제 두 권의 책을 샀다. 한 권은 '어린 왕자'이고 나머지 한 권은 '갈매기의 꿈'이다. 나는 두 권 모두 민수에게 생일 선물로 줄 것이다.

_____

_____

_____

_____

- *The Little Prince* '어린 왕자'
- *Jonathan Livingston Seagull* '갈매기의 꿈'

# Chapter 04

관계사

## Chapter 미리보기

| | | | |
|---|---|---|---|
| 관계대명사 | 사람 | who | I know the boy who likes Sue. |
| | | whose | I know the boy whose name is Tim. |
| | | whom | I know the boy whom Sue likes. |
| | 사물 · 동물 | which | This is the desk which is made of wood. |
| | | whose | This is the desk whose legs are made of iron. |
| | | which | This is the desk which he made. |
| 관계부사 | 장소 | where | I know the house where he was born. |
| | 시간 | when | I know the day when he was born. |
| | 이유 | why | I know the reason why he came here. |
| | 방법 | how | I know how he solved the problem. |

▶ 하늘은 스스로 돕는 자를 돕는다.

## Unit 08 관계대명사의 개념과 who

### A 관계대명사의 개념

관계대명사는 접속사와 대명사 역할을 하며, 종류는 다음과 같다.

|  | 주격 | 소유격 | 목적격 |
|---|---|---|---|
| 사람 | who | whose | whom |
| 사물, 동물 | which | whose (of which) | which |
| 사람, 사물, 동물 | that | × | that |

ex • I don't know the girl who is standing there. (나는 저기에 서 있는 소녀를 모른다.)
 • This is the house which he built last year. (이것은 그가 작년에 지은 집이다.)

### B who

선행사가 사람일 때 사용한다.

**1 주격 관계대명사 who** : 주어 역할을 한다.

ex • I know the boy. + He likes Karen.
 → I know the boy who likes Karen.

**2 소유격 관계대명사 whose** : 소유격 역할을 한다.

> **Tips**
> • 소유격 whose 뒤에는 명사가 온다.

ex • I know the boy. + His brother is a singer.
 → I know the boy whose brother is a singer.

**3 목적격 관계대명사 whom** : 목적어 역할을 한다.

> **Tips**
> • 목적격 관계대명사 자리에 whom 대신 who도 쓸 수 있다.

ex • I know the boy. + Karen likes him.
 → I know the boy whom Karen likes.

# Grammar Check-Up

**01** 빈칸에 알맞은 관계대명사를 쓰시오.

1) A chef is a person _____ cooks in a restaurant.

2) Where is the milk _____ was in the refrigerator?

3) She likes the man _____ she met at the party.

4) Do you know a girl _____ father is a pilot?

2) refrigerator  냉장고

**02** 관계대명사를 사용하여 다음 두 문장을 한 문장으로 쓰시오.

1) I don't like people. + They are always late.

→ _____

2) I will meet a woman. + Her husband is a movie director.

→ _____

2) husband  남편
movie director
영화 감독

**03** 다음 문장의 관계대명사에 밑줄을 긋고 우리말로 해석하시오.

1) Do you know a man who can speak English and Japanese?

→ _____

2) The woman whom you wanted to see left for France.

→ _____

**04** 우리말과 일치하도록 주어진 관계대명사를 이용하여 문장을 완성하시오.

1) 그는 아이스크림 가게에서 일하는 소녀를 좋아한다. (who)

→ He likes the girl _____.

2) 나는 긴 머리 소녀를 좋아한다. (whose)

→ I like the girl _____.

3) 네가 만났던 그 분이 나의 아버지이다. (whom)

→ The man _____.

# Unit 09 which, that

## A which

선행사가 사물, 동물일 때 사용한다.

**Tips**
• 선행사가 사물, 동물일 때 주격과 목적격에는 which를, 소유격에는 whose를 사용한다.

**1 주격과 목적격** : 주어와 목적어 역할을 한다. 주어 역할을 할 때는 which 뒤에 동사가 오며, 목적어 역할을 할 때는 〈주어 + 동사〉가 온다.

**ex** • I like stories. + They have a happy ending.
→ I like stories which have a happy ending.

• I am looking for the key. + I lost it.
→ I am looking for the key which I lost.

**2 소유격** : whose는 소유격 역할을 하며, whose 뒤에는 명사가 온다.

**ex** • She has a dog. + Its name is Mong.
→ She has a dog whose name is Mong.

## B that

선행사가 사람, 사물, 동물일 때 사용한다.

**Tips**
• 관계대명사 that은 소유격으로 쓸 수 없다.

**1** who, whom, which 대신 쓸 수 있다.

**ex** • I know the boy that/who likes Karen.
• This is a picture that/which Picasso painted.

**2** that만 사용하는 경우

1) 사람과 동물, 사람과 사물이 선행사일 때
**ex** • Look at the man and his car that are over there.

2) 선행사 앞에 서수, 최상급, the only, the very, the same 등이 올 때
**ex** • Seoul is the most beautiful city that I have ever visited.

3) something, anything, nothing, everything이 선행사일 때
**ex** • I will give you everything that you want.

O1  **빈칸에 알맞은 관계대명사를 쓰시오.**

1) She has a digital camera _____ everyone wants.

2) Look at a man and his dog _____ are running by here.

3) This is the most exciting movie _____ I have ever seen.

4) He lives in the house _____ roof is red.

O2  **관계대명사를 사용하여 다음 두 문장을 한 문장으로 쓰시오.**

1) I have a laptop computer. + My father bought it for me.

→ _____

2) This is the very camera. + I am looking for it.

→ _____

3) I have a dog. + Its tail is white.

→ _____

2) look for ~을 찾다
  the very 바로 그
3) tail 꼬리

O3  **다음 문장의 관계대명사에 밑줄을 긋고 우리말로 해석하시오.**

1) What is the title of the movie that you told me about?

→ _____

2) Do you know a restaurant in which we can have a good meal?

→ _____

2) good meal
  맛있는 식사

O4  **우리말과 일치하도록 주어진 관계대명사를 이용하여 문장을 완성하시오.**

1) 당신이 만든 음식을 가지고 오세요. (which)

→ Please bring _____.

2) 그 문제를 풀 수 있는 유일한 사람은 앤디(Andy)이다. (that)

→ The only person _____.

# what, 관계대명사의 생략

## A what

what은 선행사를 포함하고 있으므로 앞에 선행사가 없으며, the thing which/that으로 바꾸어 쓸 수 있다.

**ex**
• This is the thing. + I wanted to have it.
→ This is what I wanted to have.
→ This is the thing which/that I wanted to have.
• Did you hear what he said?
• What I wanted to have is a digital camera.

## B 관계대명사의 생략

**1 목적격 관계대명사의 생략** : 목적격 관계대명사 which, whom, that은 생략할 수 있으며, 관계대명사 다음에는 〈주어 + 동사〉가 온다.

**ex**
• I am looking for the ring (which/that) I lost here.
• Do you know the man (whom/that) Jenny got married to?

⊕ 〈전치사 + 관계대명사〉에서는 관계대명사를 생략할 수 없다.

**ex** • Do you know the man to whom Jenny got married?

**2 〈주격 관계대명사 + be동사〉 생략** : 주격 관계대명사는 생략할 수 없지만, be동사와 함께 사용될 때는 생략할 수 있다.

**ex** • The woman (who is) dancing on the stage is my sister.
• What is the language (which is) spoken in Hungary?

## C 전치사 + 관계대명사

**ex** • This is the factory which/that he works in.
→ This is the factory in which he works. (○)
→ This is the factory he works in. (○)
→ This is the factory in that he works. (×)

# Grammar Check-Up

**01** 빈칸에 알맞은 관계대명사를 쓰시오.

1) Please tell me _____ you want.

2) This is the house in _____ my father was born.

3) The roommate with _____ I live is from China.

4) _____ I need is my parents' love.

**02** 다음 문장의 관계대명사 중 생략할 수 있는 부분에 밑줄을 그으시오.

1) The building which is made of marble is very grand.

2) I like the boy who is playing soccer over there.

3) The girl whom you played with is very beautiful.

4) I gave the beggar all the money that I had.

1) marble 대리석
grand 웅장한
4) beggar 거지

**03** 다음 문장에서 생략된 말을 괄호 안에 쓰고, 우리말로 해석하시오.

1) I don't like the picture he painted.          ( _____ )

→ _____

2) Look at the mountain covered with snow.          ( _____ )

→ _____

2) be covered with
~로 덮여있다

**04** 우리말과 일치하도록 빈칸에 알맞은 말을 쓰시오.

1) 내가 갖고 싶어하는 것은 가방이다.

→ _____ is a bag.

2) 그녀가 기다리고 있는 사람은 그녀의 선생님이다.

→ The man _____ is her teacher.

# 11 관계부사

## A 관계부사의 개념

관계부사는 접속사와 부사 역할을 하며, 〈전치사 + 관계대명사〉로 바꿔 쓸 수 있다. 종류는 다음과 같다.

| 선행사 | 관계부사 |
|---|---|
| 장소(the place, the town, the country 등) | where |
| 시간(the time, the year, the month, the season 등) | when |
| 이유(the reason) | why |
| 방법(the way) | how |

**Tips**
• 전치사 + 관계대명사
= 관계부사

**ex** • Sokcho is the place. + I was born in the place.
→ Sokcho is the place where I was born.

## B 관계부사의 종류

**1 where** : 선행사는 장소를 나타낸다.

**ex** • This is the hotel where we stayed for a week.

**2 when** : 선행사는 시간을 나타낸다.

**ex** • I can't forget the day when we got married.

**3 why** : 선행사는 이유를 나타낸다.

**ex** • I don't know the reason why she failed the exam.

**4 how** : 선행사는 방법을 나타낸다. 선행사 the way와는 함께 쓰지 않고 the way나 how 중 하나만 써야 한다.

**ex** • Please tell me how you made this sandwich. (○)
= Please tell me the way you made this sandwich. (○)
= Please tell me the way how you made this sandwich. (×)

## C 전치사 + 관계대명사

관계부사로 바꿔 쓸 수 있다.

**ex** • I know the country. + He studied art in the country.
→ I know the country which he studied art in.
→ I know the country in which he studied art.
→ I know the country where he studied art.

O1 빈칸에 알맞은 관계부사를 쓰시오.

1) Sunday is the day _____ I go to the movies with my friends.

2) Tell me the restaurant _____ we can have a good meal.

3) I don't know the reason _____ she has gone to China.

O2 두 문장의 뜻이 같도록 빈칸에 알맞은 말을 쓰시오.

1) Tell me the day on which you were born.

= Tell me the day _____ you were born.

2) I don't know the reason for which she has a long face.

= I don't know the reason _____ she has a long face.

3) This is how he fixed the computer.

= This is _____ _____ he fixed the computer.

2) have a long face
우울한 얼굴을 하다

3) fix 고치다

O3 다음 문장을 우리말로 해석하시오.

1) Do you know how he folded the paper cranes?

→ _____

2) This is the reason why they lost the game.

→ _____

1) fold 접다
paper crane 종이학

O4 우리말과 일치하도록 관계부사를 이용하여 문장을 완성하시오.

1) 나는 셰익스피어(Shakespeare)가 태어난 마을을 방문하고 싶다.

→ I would like to visit the town _____.

2) 너는 빌 게이츠(Bill Gates)가 학교를 그만둔 이유를 아니?

→ Do you know the reason _____?

2) quit 그만두다

[01 - 04] 빈칸에 들어갈 알맞은 것을 고르시오.

**01** I have a sister _____ job is a fashion designer.

① who      ② whom      ③ whose
④ which      ⑤ that

**02** The man for _____ she is waiting is very tall and handsome.

① who      ② whom      ③ whose
④ which      ⑤ that

**03** This is the bus _____ goes to New York.

① who      ② whom      ③ whose
④ which      ⑤ what

**04** I am happy to do _____ I love best in the world.

① who      ③ whose      ② which
④ that      ⑤ what

**05** 빈칸에 that이 들어갈 수 없는 것을 고르시오.

① I am looking for a ring _____ I lost.
② The building _____ wall is pink is my house.
③ This is the best person _____ I have ever met.
④ Show me the book _____ you wrote last month.
⑤ This is the hospital _____ my mother works in.

**06** 다음 중 생략할 수 있는 부분에 밑줄을 그으시오.

Look at the people who are singing and dancing on the street.

**07** 빈칸에 공통으로 들어갈 알맞은 관계대명사를 쓰시오.

• My mother gives me everything _____ I want.
• The only person _____ understands me is my mother.

**08** 빈칸에 들어갈 수 없는 것을 고르시오.

Is this _____ which you are looking for?

① the key      ② the dog      ③ the book
④ the house      ⑤ the boy

**09** 밑줄 친 부분 중 생략할 수 없는 것을 고르시오.

① This is the girl whom Mike likes.
② The dress which Karen bought yesterday was too small.
③ Do you remember the place that you parked your car in?
④ Who is the first man that reached the moon?
⑤ The woman that I sat next to was very talkative.

**10** 밑줄 친 부분과 바꿔 쓸 수 있는 관계대명사를 쓰시오.

I can't believe the thing which you are saying.
( _____ )

**11** 밑줄 친 부분이 어법상 틀린 것을 고르시오.

① I have a sister that is studying abroad.
② I have lost the umbrella that you gave to me.
③ Tell me about the foreigner who Karen got married to.
④ The boy who is crossing the street is helping an old man.
⑤ The boys who is playing computer games over there look tired.

[12-13] 관계대명사를 사용하여 다음 두 문장을 한 문장으로 쓰시오.

12  The people were very kind to me. +
I met the people in America.

→ _____

_____

13  I saw a musical. +
It was called *The Phantom of the Opera*.

→ _____

_____

[14-15] 다음 중 어법상 틀린 문장을 고르시오.

14  ① Sokcho is the city which I was born in.
② Sokcho is the city I was born in.
③ Sokcho is the city that I was born in.
④ Sokcho is the city in which I was born.
⑤ Sokcho is the city in that I was born.

15  ① This is the way in which he solved the problem.
② This is the way which he solved the problem in.
③ This is the way how he solved the problem.
④ This is the way he solved the problem.
⑤ This is how he solved the problem.

16  빈칸에 공통으로 들어갈 알맞은 것을 고르시오.

•_____ did he leave for New Zealand?

•I can't forget the day _____ he left for New Zealand.

① Why      ② Where      ③ How
④ When      ⑤ Which

[17-18] 빈칸에 알맞은 관계사를 순서대로 바르게 짝지은 것을 고르시오.

17  •This is the reason _____ I am visiting you.

•Spring is the season _____ many people get married.

•There is a store _____ we can buy water and milk.

① why – where – where
② why – when – where
③ how – when – where
④ how – where – where
⑤ where – when – where

18  •The movie is about a man _____ wants to be a rock singer.

•This is the book _____ I want to buy.

•This is the girl _____ passport was stolen.

① who – which – that
② who – which – whose
③ which – that – whose
④ that – who – which
⑤ whose – who – which

[19-20] 우리말과 일치하도록 주어진 단어를 알맞게 배열하시오.

19  그가 가지고 놀고 있는 그 공은 나의 것이다.
(which, mine, the ball, with, he, is, playing, is)

→ _____

_____

20  나는 헤밍웨이가 책을 썼던 집을 방문하고 싶다.
(visit, I, want to, the house, books, where, Hemingway, wrote)

→ _____

_____

정답 및 해설 p.8

O1 다음 글의 밑줄 친 부분 중 어법상 **틀린** 것을 고르시오.

Karen visited Korea yesterday. She wanted me ① to recommend some ② places where she should go in Seoul. Here are the places. Insa-dong, ③ which is near downtown Seoul, is famous for its galleries, pottery shops and traditional tea shops. Kyeongbok Palace, ④ which was built in 1394, is the largest and most beautiful palace. There are Namdaemun and Dongdaemun markets ⑤ which is open all night. People can buy everything at a low price. Above all, Karen, who likes shopping, wanted to go to the markets.

- recommend 추천하다   - pottery shop 도자기 가게
- traditional 전통적인   - Palace 궁전

O1 다음 내용을 참고하여 보기처럼 단어의 의미를 쓰시오.

- He is trained to fly planes.
- It gives the meanings of words.
- She teaches in a school.
- It uses singing and dancing in the story.

보기   A pilot is a person who is trained to fly planes.

1) A teacher is _____

_____.

2) A dictionary is a book _____

_____.

3) A musical is a play or film _____

_____.

O2 다음 빈칸에 들어갈 말로 가장 적절한 것을 고르시오.

Once upon a time, there was a king **A**_____ wanted to be happy. He asked the wisest man **B**_____ he could be a happy man. The wise man told the king to wear the shirt of a happy man. Soldiers searched for a happy man all over the country. At last, they brought a happy man, **C**_____ had no shirt. He told the king that he was happy because he didn't care about having things.

|   | A |   | B |   | C |
|---|---|---|---|---|---|
| ① | who | – | the way how | – | who |
| ② | who | – | the way | – | which |
| ③ | who | – | how | – | who |
| ④ | whom | – | the way | – | that |
| ⑤ | whom | – | how | – | who |

O2 다음 우리말을 읽고 바르게 영작하시오.

나는 외국에 살고 있는 두 명의 친구가 있다. 파리에 살고 있는 친구는 음악을 공부하고 있다. 미국에 살고 있는 친구는 작가이다. 우리는 자주 만나지 못하지만 종종 서로 이메일을 한다.

_____

_____

_____

We seldom meet, but we often email one another.

- foreign country 외국      - Paris (프랑스의) 파리
- seldom 좀처럼 ~않다

Chapter

05

형용사·부사·비교

## Chapter 미리보기

| | | | |
|---|---|---|---|
| **부정의 수량형용사** | many, a number of, a few, few | **원급** | Jane is as kind as John. |
| | much, a great deal of, a little, little | **비교급** | David is stronger than Paul. |
| | a lot of, lots of, some, any, no | **최상급** | Ann is the cleverest student in my class. |
| **빈도부사** | always, usually, often, sometimes, never | **비교구문** | This bag is twice as big as that one. |
| | | | The more, the better. |
| **주요 동사구** | put on, take off, turn on, turn off, set up, pick up, try on, give up | | It is getting colder and colder. |
| | | | Which is faster, a turtle or a rabbit? |
| | | | Paul is one of the best actors in Canada. |

▶ 늦더라도 안 하는 것보다는 낫다.

# 12 부정의 수량형용사, 빈도부사, 주요 동사구

## A 부정의 수량형용사

부정의 수량형용사는 특정한 수나 양을 나타내지 않고 막연한 수나 양의 정도를 나타내는 형용사이다.

| | | |
|---|---|---|
| 셀 수 있는 명사 | many, a number of (많이 있는) <br> a few (조금 있는) <br> few (거의 없는) | a lot of, lots of (많은) <br> some, any (약간의) <br> no (없는) |
| 셀 수 없는 명사 | much, a great deal of (많이 있는) <br> a little (조금 있는) <br> little (거의 없는) | |

**ex** • I have many/a number of/a few/few/a lot of/lots of/some books.
- She has little/a little/a great deal of/a lot of/lots of/some water.

⊕ some은 긍정문과 권유를 나타내는 의문문에서 사용되며, any는 부정문과 의문문에서 사용된다.

**ex** • They have some books.            • Will you have some sandwiches?
- He didn't have any pens.            • Do you have any pens?

## B 빈도부사

빈도부사는 조동사와 be동사 뒤에, 일반동사 앞에 위치한다.

| | | |
|---|---|---|
| He can | 빈도부사 <br> always, usually, often, sometimes, never | help us. |
| He is | | kind. |
| He | | smiles |

## C 주요 동사구

〈동사 + 부사〉의 형태를 갖는 동사구로 목적어가 명사이면 〈동사 + 명사 + 부사〉 또는 〈동사 + 부사 + 명사〉의 어순이지만, 목적어가 대명사이면 〈동사 + 대명사 + 부사〉의 어순이 된다.

**ex** • put your coat on (○)                • put on your coat (○)
- put it on (○)                        • put on it (×)

O1 다음 중 알맞은 것을 고르시오.

1) There are  any | some  children in the playground.

2) I took off  my shoes | them  .

3) She met him  a little | a few  years ago.

4) He drank  a little | a few  milk for breakfast.

1) playground  놀이터
2) take off  벗다

O2 다음 문장의 틀린 부분에 밑줄을 긋고 바르게 고쳐 쓰시오.

1) He picked up it.                                (→ _____ )

2) She always is kind to us.                      (→ _____ )

3) There aren't some chairs in the classroom.    (→ _____ )

1) pick up  집어들다

O3 다음 문장을 우리말로 해석하시오.

1) Paul has few friends.

→ _____

2) I will never meet him again.

→ _____

3) I turned the light off.

→ _____

O4 우리말과 일치하도록 주어진 말을 알맞게 배열하시오.

1) 그녀는 그것을 사기 전에 입어 보았다.

(on, she, it, before, tried, bought, it, she)

→ _____

2) 그는 자주 야구 모자를 쓴다.

(wears, a, he, baseball, often, cap)

→ _____

# 13 원급, 비교급, 최상급

## A as + 형용사/부사 원급 + as

'~만큼 …한'이란 뜻이며, 두 개 또는 그 이상을 비교하여 양쪽이 동등한 것을 나타낸다.

**ex**
- Ann is as old as Jane.
- David talks as fast as Ann.
- This skirt is not as long as that one.
  = That skirt is longer than this one.
  = This skirt is shorter than that one.

## B 비교급 + than

'~보다 …한'이란 뜻이며, 비교 대상 중 어느 한쪽이 더 잘하거나 못하는 것 등을 나타낸다.

**Tips**
- much, far, even, a lot, still은 '훨씬'이란 뜻으로 비교급을 강조한다.

**ex**
- Jane is kinder than David.
- This question is more difficult than that one.
- Paul is much more famous than Harry.

## C the + 최상급

'가장 ~한'이란 뜻이며, 비교 대상이 가장 최고이거나 최저인 것을 나타낸다.

**Tips**
- 〈the + 최상급 + in + 장소/범위〉
- 〈the + 최상급 + of + 비교 대상〉

**ex**
- Jane is the most beautiful girl in her school.
- Ann is the smartest of all students.

## D 비교급과 최상급 만들기

| | | | |
|---|---|---|---|
| ⓐ 1음절 : -er, -est를 붙인다. | kind | kinder | kindest |
| ⓑ -y로 끝난 경우 y를 i로 고치고 -er, -est를 붙인다. | easy | easier | easiest |
| ⓒ 1음절에서 〈단모음 + 단자음〉으로 끝난 경우 마지막 자음을 한 번 더 쓰고 -er, -est를 붙인다. | hot | hotter | hottest |
| ⓓ 2음절이나 3음절 이상의 단어 앞에는 more, most를 붙인다. | interesting | more interesting | most interesting |
| ⓔ 불규칙 변화 | good/well | better | best |
| | bad/ill | worse | worst |
| | many/much | more | most |

# Grammar Check-Up

**01** 다음 중 알맞은 것을 고르시오.

1) Paul is as  nice｜nicer  as David.

2) This house is  cleaner｜cleanest  than that one.

3) Tom is the  worse｜worst  wizard in Hogwarts.

4) David is  very｜much  smarter than Ann.

3) wizard  마법사

**02** 주어진 단어의 원급, 비교급, 최상급을 이용하여 문장을 완성하시오.

1) David is ＿＿＿＿＿＿＿＿＿＿＿＿＿ as John. (happy)

2) This yacht is ＿＿＿＿＿＿＿＿＿＿＿ than that one. (good)

3) This is the ＿＿＿＿＿＿＿＿＿＿＿ car in this company. (popular)

2) yacht  요트
3) popular  인기 있는

**03** 다음 문장을 우리말로 해석하시오.

1) My laptop is not as fast as yours.

→ ＿＿＿＿＿＿＿＿＿＿＿＿＿＿＿＿＿＿＿＿＿

2) Mt. Everest is the highest mountain in the world.

→ ＿＿＿＿＿＿＿＿＿＿＿＿＿＿＿＿＿＿＿＿＿

3) *Harry Potter* is much more interesting than *Treasure Island*.

→ ＿＿＿＿＿＿＿＿＿＿＿＿＿＿＿＿＿＿＿＿＿

1) laptop  휴대용 컴퓨터
3) *Treasure Islands*  '보물섬'

**04** 우리말과 일치하도록 빈칸에 알맞은 말을 쓰시오.

1) 이 책은 저 책만큼 웃긴다.

→ This book is ＿＿＿＿＿ ＿＿＿＿＿ ＿＿＿＿＿ that one.

2) 그는 우리 학교에서 가장 현명한 학생이다.

→ He is ＿＿＿＿＿ ＿＿＿＿＿ ＿＿＿＿＿ in my school.

3) 그는 체육 선생님보다 훨씬 힘이 세다.

→ He is much ＿＿＿＿＿ ＿＿＿＿＿ my P.E. teacher.

2) wise  현명한
3) P.E. teacher  체육 선생님

# 14 비교구문

## A 배수사 (twice, three times 등) + as + 원급 + as ~

'몇 배 ~한'이란 뜻이며, 〈배수사 + 비교급 + than ~〉과 같은 뜻이다.

ex • This bag is three times as big as that one.
   = This bag is three times bigger than that one.

## B the + 비교급 (주어 + 동사), the + 비교급 (주어 + 동사)

'~할수록 …하다'라는 뜻이다.

ex • The more, the better.
   • The faster you walk, the earlier you will get there.

## C 비교급 + and + 비교급

'점점 더 ~한'이란 뜻이다.

ex • It is getting colder and colder.
   • Her hair is getting longer and longer.

━⊕ famous, popular, slowly 등 긴 음절에서는 〈more and more + 형용사〉로 표현한다.

   ex • The singer is becoming more and more famous. (O)
      • The singer is becoming more famous and more famous. (×)

## D Which/Who ~ + 비교급, A or B?

'A와 B 중 어느 것이/누가 더 ~한가?'라는 뜻이다.

ex • Which is faster, a turtle or a rabbit?
   • Who is taller, Jane or Ann?

## E one of the + 최상급 + 복수명사

'가장 ~한 사람들/것들 중의 하나'라는 뜻이다.

ex • Jane is one of the most diligent students in our class.

# Grammar Check-Up

정답 및 해설 p.9

**01** 주어진 단어를 알맞은 형태로 바꾸어 빈칸에 쓰시오.

1) He is becoming _____ and _____. (weak)

2) This building is three times _____ than that one. (high)

3) He is one of the _____ _____ in the world.
(lucky, man)

**02** 다음 문장의 <u>틀린</u> 부분에 밑줄을 긋고 바르게 고쳐 쓰시오.

1) The most you have, the more you want.  (→ _____ )

2) This room is four times as bigger as that one.  (→ _____ )

3) Who is more stubborn, Jane and David?  (→ _____ )

3) stubborn  고집이 센

**03** 다음 문장을 우리말로 해석하시오.

1) This ship is three times as large as that one.

→ _____

2) The more you exercise, the healthier you will be.

→ _____

3) Knowing English is getting more and more important.

→ _____

2) healthy  건강한

**04** 우리말과 일치하도록 빈칸에 알맞은 말을 쓰시오.

1) 빠르면 빠를수록 좋다.

→ The _____, the _____.

2) 이 복도는 저 복도보다 두 배가 넓다.

→ This hallway is _____ _____
_____ _____ that one.

3) 그는 가장 위대한 작곡가 중의 한 명이다.

→ He is _____ of _____ _____
_____.

2) hallway  복도
3) composer  작곡가

O1 주어진 단어를 알맞은 형태로 바꾸어 빈칸에 쓰시오.

> A: Ann won the gold medal at the 2004 Olympic Games.
>
> B: I know. She is the _____ gymnast in the world. (good)

[02-03] 다음 표를 보고 주어진 단어를 알맞은 형태로 바꾸어 빈칸에 쓰시오.

|  | height | weight |
|---|---|---|
| Ann | 155cm | 50kg |
| Jane | 155cm | 48kg |

O2 Jane is _____ _____ _____ Ann. (tall)

O3 Ann is _____ _____ Jane. (heavy)

O4 우리말과 일치하도록 빈칸에 알맞은 말을 쓰시오.

> 그 배우는 점점 더 유명해지고 있다.
> → The actor is becoming _____ _____ _____ _____.

O5 빈칸에 공통으로 들어갈 알맞은 것을 고르시오.

> • Jane has _____ Korean friends.
> • Jane drank _____ apple juice.

① much　② many　③ a lot of
④ a few　⑤ a little

O6 두 문장이 같은 뜻이 되도록 빈칸에 알맞은 말을 쓰시오.

> Ann doesn't sing as well as Paul.
> = Paul sings _____ _____ Ann.

O7 빈칸에 들어갈 알맞은 것을 고르시오.

> Vatican City is one of the _____ in the world.

① smallest country　② smaller country
③ smallest countries　④ smaller countries
⑤ small country

[08-09] 우리말과 일치하도록 빈칸에 알맞은 말을 쓰시오.

O8 날씨가 더워질수록, 우리는 아이스크림을 더 많이 먹는다.
> → The _____ it is, the _____ ice cream we eat.

O9 그는 내가 가진 것보다 두 배 많은 만화책을 가지고 있다.
> → He has _____ _____ many comics as I have.

O10 빈칸에 들어갈 수 **없는** 것을 고르시오.

> She has _____ more friends than he has.

① much　② far　③ very
④ a lot　⑤ even

11 빈칸에 알맞은 단어를 순서대로 바르게 짝지은 것을 고르시오.

> Which is _____, an airplane _____ a train?

① faster – and
② faster – but
③ faster – or
④ fast – and
⑤ fast – or

[12-13] 빈칸에 공통으로 들어갈 알맞은 말을 쓰시오.

12 • John doesn't have _____ friends.
• Do you have _____ questions?

13 • It is becoming _____ and more interesting.
• Babies cry _____ than we do.

14 주어진 말을 알맞은 곳에 넣어 문장을 다시 쓰시오.

> He meets her to go to the movies. (often)

→ He _____.

15 두 문장의 뜻이 같지 않은 것을 고르시오.

① This box is twice as heavy as that one.
= This box is twice heavier than that one.
② Winter is the coldest season.
= Winter is colder than any other season.
③ This bag is bigger than that one.
= That bag is smaller than this one.
④ Ann's hair is longer than Jane's.
= Jane's hair is as long as Ann's.
⑤ David is not as quiet as John.
= John is quieter than David.

16 밑줄 친 부분이 어법상 틀린 것을 고르시오.

① She is the cleverest student in her class.
② I can run faster than Ann.
③ It is getting hotter and hotter here.
④ This plant is twice as short as that one.
⑤ This is one of the oldest palace in Seoul.

[17-19] 다음 중 어법상 틀린 문장을 고르시오.

17 ① She turned the light off.
② She turned on the light.
③ She picked it up.
④ She took off it.
⑤ She put them on.

18 ① She is sometimes late for school.
② He never goes to the library.
③ We will always remember our teacher.
④ I visit often my grandparents.
⑤ They usually have dinner at home.

19 ① There is little apple juice in the bottle.
② She has a lot of toys.
③ There is a few books.
④ We don't have much money.
⑤ He took a few photos.

20 보기와 같은 뜻의 문장을 고르시오.

> 보기 My puppy weighs 5kg and your puppy weighs 6kg.

① My puppy is heavier than yours.
② Your puppy is not as heavy as mine.
③ My puppy is the heavier of the two.
④ Your puppy is heavier than mine.
⑤ My puppy is as heavy as yours.

정답 및 해설 p.10

O1 다음 글의 밑줄 친 부분 중 어법상 틀린 것을 고르시오.

> Jane is ① one of the most beautiful girls in our school. She is also ② the most popular girl in our school. Every boy wants to go out with her. Her sister, Ann, is ③ as pretty as Jane. Some say that Ann is ④ very more attractive than Jane. They are quite different. Ann is very shy but Jane is very outgoing. Ann likes ⑤ studying but Jane likes playing sports.

- go out with ~와 데이트하다
- attractive 매력적인
- outgoing 외향적인

O1 다음 그림을 보고 형용사 expensive를 이용하여 빈칸에 알맞은 말을 쓰시오.

1) A is _____ _____ as _____ as D.

2) C is _____ _____ expensive _____ B.

3) C is _____ expensive _____ D.

4) D is _____ cheaper _____ A.

O2 다음 괄호 안에서 어법에 맞는 표현으로 가장 적절한 것을 고르시오.

> Ann is a bit of a bookworm. She reads seven books a week. She reads Ⓐ (much and much / more and more) books. The more she reads books, Ⓑ (the most / the more) she wants to read. She has four times Ⓒ (as many books as / as more books as) I have. Her favorite book is *The fastest reader in the world*.

     Ⓐ        Ⓑ        Ⓒ

① much and much – the most – as many books as

② much and much – the more – as more books as

③ more and more – the more – as more books as

④ more and more – the most – as many books as

⑤ more and more – the more – as many books as

O2 다음 우리말을 읽고 바르게 영작하시오.

마이클(Michael)은 미국 최고의 가수 중 한 명이다. 그는 존(John)보다 춤을 훨씬 더 잘 춘다. 그는 전 세계에서 점점 더 유명해지고 있다.

_____

_____

_____

_____

Chapter

# 06

문장의 형식

## Chapter 미리보기

| | |
|---|---|
| **주어** | 문장의 주체이며, '~은, ~는, ~이, ~가'로 해석한다. |
| **동사** | 주어의 동작이나 상태를 나타내며, '~다'로 해석한다. |
| **목적어** | 동사가 나타내는 행위의 대상이 되는 것을 가리키며, '~을, ~를, ~에게'로 해석한다. |
| **보어** | 주어나 목적어를 보충 설명한다. |
| **1형식** | 주어 + 동사 |
| **2형식** | 주어 + 동사 + 주격 보어 |
| **3형식** | 주어 + 동사 + 목적어 |
| **4형식** | 주어 + 동사 + 간접목적어 + 직접목적어 |
| **5형식** | 주어 + 동사 + 목적어 + 목적격 보어 |

The early bird catches the worm. 일찍 일어나는 새가 벌레를 잡는다.

▶ 부지런하면 성공한다.

## A | 주어

문장의 주체이며, '~은, ~는, ~이, ~가'로 해석한다. 일반적으로 명사나 대명사가 주어 자리에 온다.

ex • She likes flowers.
   • Julie is talking with her friend.

## B | 동사

주어의 동작이나 상태를 나타내며, '~다'로 해석한다.

ex • My sister was late this morning.
   • He enjoyed his holiday.

## C | 목적어

동사가 나타내는 행위의 대상이 되는 것을 가리키며, '~을, ~를, ~에게'로 해석한다. 명사나 대명사가 목적어 자리에 오며, 간접목적어와 직접목적어로 나눌 수 있다. 간접목적어는 '~에게'로, 직접목적어는 '~을, 를'로 해석한다.

ex • She saw me.
   • Charlie speaks German.
   • Lucy showed her friend some pictures.
            간접목적어      직접목적어

## D | 보어

주어나 목적어를 보충 설명하며, 주로 명사나 형용사가 보어 자리에 온다.

1 **주격 보어** : 주어를 설명해 준다.

   ex • She is a dentist. (She = a dentist)
      • She looks happy. (She → happy )

2 **목적격 보어** : 목적어를 설명해 준다.

   ex • We call him Brian. (him = Brian)
      • She made him happy. (him → happy)

01  밑줄 친 부분에 해당하는 문장 요소를 괄호 안에 쓰시오.

1) My mother made us some pizza.              (→ _____ )

2) I found him honest.                        (→ _____ )

3) She is a flight attendant.                 (→ _____ )

2) honest  정직한

3) flight attendant
비행기 승무원

02  보기와 같이 다음 문장을 문장 요소로 구분하여 표시하시오.

> 보기  J. K. Rowling became a famous writer.
>        주어       동사       보어

1) J. K. Rowling wrote *Harry Potter*.

2) Harry sent his friend a letter.

2) send (– sent – sent)
보내다

03  다음 문장을 우리말로 해석하시오.

1) My father bought me a computer.

→ _____

2) His parents call him Tommy.

→ _____

04  다음 우리말을 영작하시오.

1) 그녀는 어제 매우 피곤해 보였다.

→ _____

2) 그들은 호텔을 짓는 중이다.

→ _____

# 1, 2, 3형식 문장

## A | 1형식 문장

〈주어 + 동사〉

**ex** • Sue dances.
　　　주어　동사

• There are some flowers in the garden.
　　동사　　주어　　　　　수식어

• My mother gets up early.

## B | 2형식 문장

〈주어 + 동사 + 주격 보어〉

**ex** • Today is Monday. (Today = Monday)
　　　주어　동사　주격 보어

• Your mother is very beautiful. (Your mother → very beautiful)

⊕ 〈감각동사(look, feel, sound, taste, smell 등) + 형용사〉

**ex** • You look happy.
　　• The flower smells good.
　　• Silk feels soft.

〈get/grow/become + 비교급 + and + 비교급〉 '점점 더 ~해지다'

**ex** • She is getting prettier and prettier.
　　• The days are getting shorter and shorter.

## C | 3형식 문장

〈주어 + 동사 + 목적어〉

**ex** • My sister cleans the house.
　　　주어　　　동사　　목적어

• Everybody enjoyed the party.
• She likes them.
• She saw herself in the mirror.

○1 **다음 중 알맞은 것을 고르시오.**

1) Your wife looks   happy ㅣ happily ㅣ happiness  .

2) They invited   us ㅣ we ㅣ our   yesterday.

3) I feel   sleep ㅣ sleepy  .

○2 **우리말과 일치하도록 주어진 말을 알맞게 배열하시오.**

1) 수는 축구를 좋아하지 않는다. (soccer, like, doesn't, Sue)

→ _____

2) 나는 매일 커피 두 잔을 마신다. (two, drink, every, cups of coffee, day, I)

→ _____

3) 해는 동쪽에서 뜬다. (in the east, the sun, rises)

→ _____

*3) rise  뜨다, 떠오르다*

○3 **다음 문장을 우리말로 해석하시오.**

1) The world is getting smaller and smaller.

→ _____

2) Tim bought a golden ring yesterday.

→ _____

*2) golden ring  금반지*

○4 **다음 우리말을 영작하시오.**

1) 그녀는 항상 슬퍼 보인다.

→ _____

2) 그녀는 어제 서울을 떠났다.

→ _____

3) 그는 그의 차 안에 있다.

→ _____

# 17 4, 5형식 문장

## A 4형식 문장

〈주어 + 동사 + 간접목적어 + 직접목적어〉

ex • Karen  gave  Alice  the book.
　　　주어　동사　간·목　　직·목
• Brian sent me an email.
• She bought me a pretty card.

⊕ 4형식 문장을 3형식 문장으로 바꿀 때 동사에 따라 간접목적어 앞에 전치사 to, for, of를 쓴다.

| ⓐ 전치사 to를 쓰는 동사 | give, send, write, tell, show 등 |
| ⓑ 전치사 for를 쓰는 동사 | buy, make, get 등 |
| ⓒ 전치사 of를 쓰는 동사 | ask 등 |

ex • Tim wrote his fans postcards.
→ Tim wrote postcards to his fans.
• The teacher told us a story.
→ The teacher told a story to us.
• He showed me his photos.
→ He showed his photos to me.
• He made her a bookcase.
→ He made a bookcase for her.
• I asked my math teacher a question.
→ I asked a question of my math teacher.

## B 5형식 문장

〈주어 + 동사 + 목적어 + 목적격 보어〉

ex • They  call  me  Mong. (me = Mong)
　　　주어　동사　목적어　목·보
• The movie made him a famous actor. (him = a famous actor)
• He found her honest. (her → honest)

◯1 다음 중 알맞은 것을 고르시오.

1) Please show  my │ me │ I  your notebook.

2) Minyeong wrote a letter  for │ of │ to  her parents.

3) His song made me  happy │ happily │ happiness  .

◯2 우리말과 일치하도록 주어진 말을 알맞게 배열하시오.

1) 우리는 그녀를 대통령으로 선출했다. (president, her, we, elected)

→ _____

2) 그는 나에게 책상을 만들어 주었다. (me, he, made, a desk)

→ _____

1) president  대통령
    elect  선출하다

◯3 두 문장의 뜻이 같도록 빈칸에 알맞은 말을 쓰시오.

1) I asked her some questions.

= I asked some questions _____ _____.

2) She bought him a key holder.

= She bought a key holder _____ _____.

2) key holder
    열쇠고리

◯4 다음 문장을 우리말로 해석하시오.

1) Mr. and Mrs. Smith will make their son a dentist.

→ _____

2) Mr. and Mrs. Smith will make their son a model plane.

→ _____

2) model plane
    모형 비행기

◯5 다음 우리말을 영작하시오.

1) 그녀는 우리에게 영어를 가르친다.

→ _____

2) 우리는 그녀를 베키(Becky)라고 부른다.

→ _____

[01-04] 빈칸에 들어갈 수 <u>없는</u> 것을 고르시오.

O1    He made her _____.

① a chair    ② happy    ③ angry
④ a doll    ⑤ sadly

O2    Karen looks _____.

① kindly    ② lovely    ③ cute
④ pretty    ⑤ young

O3    She always tells _____ an interesting story.

① him    ② Brian    ③ us
④ their    ⑤ her brother

O4    She visited _____ last weekend.

① America    ② me    ③ Sue
④ in Seoul    ⑤ her grandfather

[05-06] 우리말과 일치하도록 빈칸에 알맞은 말을 쓰시오.

O5    그는 나에게 장미 한 송이를 사 주었다.
→ He bought _____ a rose.
→ He bought _____ _____
_____ _____.

O6    나는 부모님께 편지를 썼다.
→ I wrote my _____ _____
_____.
→ I wrote _____ _____
_____ _____.

[07-08] 빈칸에 들어갈 알맞은 전치사를 고르시오.

O7    Sue showed a laptop computer _____ me.

① of    ② on    ③ for
④ to    ⑤ in

O8    May I ask a favor _____ you?

① of    ② on    ③ for
④ to    ⑤ in

O9    빈칸에 들어갈 알맞은 것을 고르시오.

You will _____ a famous pianist.

① look    ② feel    ③ become
④ sound    ⑤ go

[10-12] 우리말과 일치하도록 주어진 단어를 알맞게 배열하시오.

1O    우리는 고양이 이름을 제리로 지었다.
(Jerry, named, the cat, we)
→ _____

11    그는 우리에게 거짓말을 했다.
(us, a lie, told, he)
→ _____

12    나는 학교에서 많은 것을 배웠다.
(learned, a lot of, I, things, at school)
→ _____

13 보기와 문장의 형식이 <u>다른</u> 것을 고르시오.

보기  She is getting prettier and prettier.

① Sue became an English teacher.
② Today is Sunday.
③ The food tastes salty.
④ Tim is very handsome.
⑤ Brian dances very well.

14 보기와 문장의 형식이 같은 것을 고르시오.

보기  He gave her a bunch of flowers.

① I drink too much coke.
② My friend calls her daughter Yuri.
③ He made me a singer.
④ Please pass me the salt.
⑤ He gave a bunch of flowers to me.

15 다음 중 올바른 문장을 고르시오.

① That sounds strangely.
② Karen gave apple juice Sue.
③ Please keep your feet warmly.
④ He teaches us to math.
⑤ Kimchi tastes hot.

16 빈칸에 들어갈 알맞은 것을 <u>두 개</u> 고르시오.

He _____ a kite for me.

① gave       ② showed       ③ made
④ lent       ⑤ bought

17 다음 중 어법상 <u>틀린</u> 문장을 고르시오.

① He closed the door quietly.
② The sun sets in the west.
③ I found him honestly.
④ I forgot her name.
⑤ This lotion smells bad.

[18-20] 우리말과 일치하도록 빈칸에 알맞은 말을 쓰시오.

18 날씨가 점점 추워지고 있다.

→ It is getting _____ _____

_____.

19 그는 그녀에게 아름다운 드레스를 만들어 주었다.

→ He made a beautiful _____

_____ _____.

20 그녀는 매일 밤 그녀의 딸에게 책을 읽어 주었다.

→ She read _____ _____ _____

_____ every night.

O1 다음 글의 밑줄 친 부분 중 어법상 틀린 것을 고르시오.

Children! Take off those dirty clothes and ① put on some clean ones. ② Give the dirty ones me. Now pick up your toys and put them away. Put the trash in the trash can. Please ③ keep your room clean. You can't watch TV until you ④ do your homework. Turn off the television. Now tell me about your classes today. Tim! ⑤ What are you doing?

■ take off 벗다    ■ put on 입다    ■ put away 치우다

O2 다음 괄호 안에서 어법에 맞는 표현으로 가장 적절한 것을 고르시오.

Today is Parents' Day. We gave a carnation and some presents A (to / for) our parents. My brother bought two pairs of socks B (to / for) my father. I bought my mother a hairpin. Also, I made lunch C (for / of) them and my brother washed the dishes. My father suggested that we should eat out in the evening. We had Bulgogi for dinner. It is my favorite food. I was very full. On the way home, my mother bought a cheesecake that I liked. My family had it as a dessert at home. Today was a really nice day.

■ suggest 제안하다    ■ on the way home 집에 가는 도중에

|  | A |  | B |  | C |
|---|---|---|---|---|---|
| ① | to | – | to | – | of |
| ② | to | – | for | – | of |
| ③ | to | – | for | – | for |
| ④ | for | – | for | – | of |
| ⑤ | for | – | to | – | of |

O1 다음 그림을 보고 보기의 단어들을 이용하여 빈칸에 알맞은 말을 쓰시오.

보기  bought     for     to     sent
      a Christmas card    a bunch of flowers

1)
Brian _____

_____ Minyeong.

2)
I _____

_____ Chris.

O2 다음 우리말을 읽고 바르게 영작하시오.

하루 종일 비가 왔다. 아이들은 밖에 나가지 못했다. 그들은 지루해 보였다. 나는 그들에게 떡을 만들어 주었다. 그것은 그들을 기쁘게 했다.

_____

_____

_____

_____

_____

■ all day long 하루 종일    ■ rice cake 떡

# Chapter 07

to부정사

Unit 18 명사적 용법
Unit 19 형용사적 용법, 부사적 용법
Unit 20 to부정사의 의미상 주어
Unit 21 지각동사, 사역동사

## Chapter 미리보기

| | | |
|---|---|---|
| **명사적 용법** | 주어 | It is not easy to speak English. |
| | 보어 | My hobby is to collect old books. |
| | 목적어 | I decided to go to Canada. |
| **형용사적 용법** | 명사 + to 동사원형 | I have something to eat. |
| | 명사 + to 동사원형 + 전치사 | I need a pen to write with. |
| **부사적 용법** | 목적 | I went to the library to read some books. |
| | 감정의 원인 | I am excited to hear the news. |
| | 결과 | She lived to be one hundred years old. |
| | 형용사 수식 | This book is easy to read. |
| **의미상 주어** | ⟨difficult, easy, impossible + for⟩, ⟨kind, nice, wise + of⟩ | |
| **지각, 사역동사** | see, feel, hear, listen to, let, make, have + 목적어 + 동사원형 | |

To teach a fish how to swim 물고기에게 수영법 가르치기

▶ 공자 앞에서 문자 쓰기, 번데기 앞에서 주름잡기

## Unit 18 명사적 용법

**Tips**

• to부정사가 명사로 사용되어 주어, 목적어, 보어 역할을 한다.

• to부정사의 부정은 〈not + to부정사〉로 표현한다.

### A | 주어 역할

**ex** • To play with friends is fun.
= It is fun to play with friends.
• To study English every day is not easy.
= It is not easy to study English every day.

### B | 목적어 역할

**ex** • I want to eat pizza.
• She decided to take an English exam.
• I decided not to go to Canada.
• He is planning to go to London.

### C | 보어 역할

**ex** • Her dream is to become a scientist.
• My wish is to travel around the world.

| | | | |
|---|---|---|---|
| what + to부정사 | 무엇을 ~할지 | I know what to do. | |
| when + to부정사 | 언제 ~할지 | We don't know when to leave. | |
| where + to부정사 | 어디로 ~할지 | She asked me where to go. | |
| how + to부정사 | 어떻게 ~할지, ~하는 방법 | He told me how to open it. | |

〈의문사 + to부정사〉는 〈의문사 + 주어 + should + 동사원형〉으로 바꿔 쓸 수 있다. 단, 〈why + to부정사〉는 사용하지 않는다.

**ex** • I don't know what to do.
→ I don't know what I should do.
• They asked me when to start.
→ They asked me when they should start.
• Kate wanted to know where to sit.
→ Kate wanted to know where she should sit.
• Kevin knew how to use the machine.
→ Kevin knew how he should use the machine.

정답 및 해설 p.12

**01** 밑줄 친 to부정사의 역할(주어/목적어/보어)을 쓰시오.

1) It is difficult to forgive your enemy.　　　(→ _____ )

2) They decided to move to Busan.　　　(→ _____ )

3) Her dream is to become an astronaut.　　　(→ _____ )

1) forgive 용서하다
　 enemy 적
3) astronaut 우주비행사

**02** 다음 문장의 **틀린** 부분에 밑줄을 긋고 바르게 고쳐 쓰시오.

1) We want going to an ice rink.　　　(→ _____ )

2) I know where finding it.　　　(→ _____ )

3) Her hobby is play the violin.　　　(→ _____ )

1) ice rink 스케이트장

**03** to부정사에 주의하여 다음 문장을 우리말로 해석하시오.

1) It is hard to open this bottle.

→ _____

2) She knew how to fix it.

→ _____

3) Dad planned not to smoke.

→ _____

2) fix 고치다

**04** 우리말과 일치하도록 주어진 말을 바르게 배열하시오.

1) 그는 그녀를 언제 만날지 모른다. (when, doesn't, he, her, meet, know, to)

→ _____

2) 그녀는 그를 만나지 않기로 결심했다. (decided, she, to, him, meet, not)

→ _____

3) 그의 직업은 기념품을 파는 것이다. (sell, is, his, souvenirs, job, to)

→ _____

3) souvenir 기념품

# 19 형용사적 용법, 부사적 용법

## A 형용사적 용법

to부정사가 형용사 역할을 하여 명사나 대명사를 수식하며, '〜하는, 〜할'로 해석한다.

### 1 〈명사 + to부정사〉

ex ▶
- She has a book to read.
- I have something to do.
- It is time to go to bed.

<blockquote>
**Tips**
- 〈It is time + to부정사〉
는 '〜할 시간이다'라는
뜻이다.
</blockquote>

### 2 〈명사 + to부정사 + 전치사〉

ex ▶
- I have some friends to play with. (○)
- I have some friends to play. (×)

## B 부사적 용법

to부정사가 부사 역할을 하여 형용사, 부사, 동사를 수식한다.

### 1 목적 (〜하기 위하여)

ex ▶
- We went to a restaurant to (= in order to) have lunch.
- He saved some money to buy a new MP3 player.

<blockquote>
**Tips**
- 감정을 나타내는 형용
사에는 happy, glad,
pleased, excited 등
이 있다.
</blockquote>

### 2 감정의 원인 (〜해서, 〜하니)

ex ▶
- I am happy to see you again.
- He is excited to watch the football game.

### 3 결과 (〜해서 …하다)

ex ▶
- They grew up to be scientists.

### 4 형용사 수식 (〜하기에)

ex ▶
- This English book is easy to read.

O1 밑줄 친 to부정사의 용법(형용사/부사)을 쓰시오.

1) She goes to the bakery to buy a loaf of bread. (→ _____ )

2) She doesn't have anything to eat. (→ _____ )

3) He was surprised to find her at the gymnasium. (→ _____ )

1) a loaf of bread
빵 한 덩어리

3) gymnasium
체육관

O2 다음 중 알맞은 것을 고르시오.

1) I have a piece of paper  to write | to write on  .

2) He doesn't have any friends  to play | to play with  .

3) There are some books  to read | to read with  .

4) I have a lot of homework  to do | to do with  .

O3 다음 문장을 우리말로 해석하시오.

1) The antique vase is easy to break.

→ _____

2) She needs some friends to talk to.

→ _____

3) My grandmother lived to be 94 years old.

→ _____

1) antique vase
골동품 화병

O4 우리말과 일치하도록 빈칸에 알맞은 말을 쓰시오.

1) 나는 쓸 펜이 필요하다.

→ I need a pen _____ _____ _____.

2) 우리는 친척을 만나서 기뻤다.

→ We were pleased _____ _____ our relatives.

3) 그녀는 유럽에 가기 위하여 돈을 모으고 있다.

→ She's saving some money _____ _____
_____ _____.

2) relative  친척

# to부정사의 의미상 주어

## A 진주어와 가주어

to부정사가 주어 역할을 하는 경우 주어가 길기 때문에 문장 뒤로 보내고 빈 주어 자리에는 아무 뜻이 없는 it을 쓰는데, 이때의 주어 it을 가주어라 하며, to부정사구는 진주어라 한다.

**ex** • To solve the puzzle is not easy.

= It is not easy to solve the puzzle.
  가주어                진주어

## B to부정사의 의미상 주어

1 **for + 목적격** : to부정사의 의미상 주어와 문장의 주어가 다르면 to부정사 앞에 일반적으로 〈for + 목적격〉을 to부정사의 의미상 주어로 사용한다.

| 가주어 | 동사 | 형용사 | 전치사 | 부정사의 의미상 주어 | 진주어(to부정사) |
|---|---|---|---|---|---|
| It | is | difficult<br>impossible<br>important | for | you/her/him/me/us/them | to speak English.<br>to read Russian.<br>to write Chinese. |

**ex** • It was not difficult for me to answer the question.
     • It is important for you to keep your promises.

2 **of + 목적격** : 사람의 성질을 나타내는 형용사에는 〈of + 목적격〉을 to부정사의 의미상 주어로 사용한다.

| 가주어 | 동사 | 형용사 | 전치사 | 부정사의 의미상 주어 | 진주어 |
|---|---|---|---|---|---|
| It | is | kind/nice/wise/<br>foolish/careful/silly | of | you/her/him/me/us/them | to do it. |

**ex** • It is nice of her to invite them to her birthday party.
     • It is silly of her to make such a mistake.

01 빈칸에 of나 for를 써 넣으시오.

1) It is wise _____ you to study hard.

2) It is important _____ me to pass the test.

3) It is easy _____ us to answer the question.

02 두 문장의 뜻이 같도록 빈칸에 알맞은 말을 쓰시오.

1) To play with matches is not safe.

= It _____.

2) To read Chinese is not easy.

= It _____.

3) To knit our own gloves is a good idea.

= It _____.

1) match 성냥

3) knit 짜다

03 다음 문장을 우리말로 해석하시오.

1) It is kind of them to do so.

→ _____

2) It is foolish of her to trust him.

→ _____

2) trust 신뢰하다

04 우리말과 일치하도록 빈칸에 알맞은 말을 쓰시오.

1) 아랍어를 말하는 것은 쉽지 않다.

→ It's _____ _____ _____
_____ Arabic.

2) 그녀가 그것을 하는 것은 불가능하다.

→ It's _____ _____ _____
_____ _____ that.

3) 와주셔서 감사합니다.

→ It is nice _____ you _____ _____.

# 21 지각동사, 사역동사

## A 동사 + 목적어 + to 동사원형

want, ask, tell, expect와 같은 동사는 목적격 보어로 to부정사를 사용한다.

| want<br>ask + 목적어 + to 동사원형<br>tell | She wants me to be a doctor.<br>I asked him to help me.<br>Mom told me to study hard. |
| --- | --- |

**ex** • I want you do it. (×)

## B 지각동사

see, hear, listen, feel, smell과 같은 지각동사는 목적격 보어로 동사원형을 사용한다.

| see, hear,<br>feel, listen to, + 목적어 + 동사원형<br>smell | I saw her laugh.<br>She heard him cry.<br>He felt someone look at him. |
| --- | --- |

**ex** • I saw him to talk to her. (×)

## C 사역동사

let, make, have와 같은 사역동사는 목적격 보어로 동사원형을 사용한다.

| let<br>make + 목적어 + 동사원형<br>have | Let me introduce myself.<br>He made her shout at him.<br>She had him clean the room. |
| --- | --- |

**ex** • They made me to feel happy. (×)

➖⊕ 지각동사는 목적격 보어로 현재분사를 사용할 수 있지만 사역동사는 사용할 수 없다.

**ex** • He heard her singing. (O)
   • He made her waiting for an hour. (×)

O1 다음 중 알맞은 것을 고르시오.

1) I want you   to leave | leave .

2) She heard him   to yell | yell .

3) He made her   to cook | cook   for him.

4) She will let us   know | knowing   our grades.

2) yell  소리치다

O2 주어진 단어를 알맞은 형태로 바꾸어 빈칸에 쓰시오.

1) I smelled something _____. (burn)

2) She told me _____ my homework. (do)

3) He made her _____ down. (fall)

1) burn  타다
3) fall down  넘어지다

O3 다음 문장을 우리말로 해석하시오.

1) I asked him to come to my recital.

  → _____

2) He saw me give a present to her.

  → _____

3) She made him feel sad.

  → _____

1) recital 독주회

O4 우리말과 일치하도록 빈칸에 알맞은 말을 쓰시오.

1) 엄마는 내가 변호사가 되기를 바라신다.

  → Mom wants _____ _____ _____

    _____ _____.

2) 나는 그가 웃는 것을 들었다.

  → I heard _____ _____.

3) 그는 우리에게 교실을 청소하도록 시켰다.

  → He had _____ _____ _____

    _____.

1) lawyer  변호사

# 내신 족집게 문제

[01-03] 주어진 단어를 알맞은 형태로 바꾸어 빈칸에 쓰시오.

01  It is relaxing _____ to music.
                        (listen)

02  My uncle decided _____ for the
    job.                        (apply)

03  Jane is really happy _____ an
    antique shop.                (open)

[04-05] 우리말과 일치하도록 빈칸에 알맞은 말을 쓰시오.

04  앤은 같이 놀 친구가 필요하다.
    → Ann needs a friend _____ _____
      _____.

05  제인, 너에게 줄 것이 아무것도 없어.
    → Jane, I have _____ _____
      _____ you.

06  빈칸에 들어갈 알맞은 것을 두 개 고르시오.

    She saw them _____.

    ① to fight     ② fought     ③ fight
    ④ will fight   ⑤ fighting

[07-09] 빈칸에 들어갈 알맞은 것을 고르시오.

07  He made me _____ happy.

    ① to feel     ② felt        ③ will feel
    ④ feel        ⑤ feeling

08  Mom wants me _____ the English contest.

    ① to win      ② won         ③ will win
    ④ win         ⑤ winning

09  Her job is _____ clothes.

    ① make        ② made        ③ to make
    ④ to making   ⑤ to made

10  빈칸에 들어갈 알맞은 말을 쓰시오.

    It is difficult _____ her to keep her
    promise.

11  빈칸에 들어갈 수 없는 것을 고르시오.

    Ann _____ to go to Canada to study
    English.

    ① wished      ② planned     ③ wanted
    ④ gave up     ⑤ hoped

12  밑줄 친 부분을 지시대로 바꾸어 문장을 다시 쓰시오.

    She told him to go to the bookstore.
    부정문 ▶ _____

**13** 다음 두 문장을 한 문장으로 나타낼 때 빈칸에 들어갈 알맞은 말을 쓰시오.

> She has a puppy. + She has to look after the puppy.
>
> → She has a puppy _____ _____
>   _____.

**14** 보기의 밑줄 친 to부정사와 용법이 같은 것을 고르시오.

> 보기  We went to the bookstore to buy textbooks.

① I was surprised to see him there.
② He has something to drink.
③ She grew up to become a singer.
④ This machine is easy to handle.
⑤ They came to my house to have lunch together.

**[15-16]** 밑줄 친 to부정사의 용법이 나머지와 다른 것을 고르시오.

**15** ① I have someone to talk to.
② She has nothing to eat.
③ There is a radio to listen to.
④ We went to Tim's house to help him.
⑤ There are some chairs to sit on.

**16** ① It is difficult to read French.
② We planned to go hiking.
③ Her dream is to travel around Brazil.
④ She has some books to read.
⑤ She wanted to go to bed early last night.

**[17-18]** 다음 중 어법상 틀린 문장을 고르시오.

**17** ① John asked her to go for lunch.
② I want him to do it.
③ Mom told me to clean my room.
④ She heard someone singing.
⑤ He made me feeling happy.

**18** ① She expected meeting him at the party.
② It is nice of you to invite him.
③ I need a pencil to write with.
④ It is interesting to read a novel.
⑤ He didn't know where to go.

**19** 대화의 빈칸에 알맞은 말을 쓰시오.

> A: What a nice MP3 player! Is it yours?
> B: Yes, it is. But I don't know _____ to use it.

**20** 두 문장의 뜻이 같지 않은 것을 고르시오.

① He sat on the sofa to take a rest.
   = He sat on the sofa in order to take a rest.
② It is kind of him to help her.
   = He is kind to help her.
③ She hopes to get a perfect score, so she is studying hard.
   = She is studying hard not to get a perfect score.
④ To play with matches is not safe.
   = It is not safe to play with matches.
⑤ I don't know what to buy for her.
   = I don't know what I should buy for her.

정답 및 해설 p.13

**O1** 다음 글의 밑줄 친 부분 중 어법상 틀린 것을 고르시오.

> In 1847, Bell ① was born in Scotland. His father was a linguist. Bell was also interested in sounds and speech. His family moved to America in 1870. There he began ② teaching deaf students. He wanted ③ help them, so he tried ④ to invent a machine to improve their hearing. While making the machine, he found he could use electricity ⑤ to send the human voice. After several experiments, Bell finally could send speech through a wire in 1876.

- linguist 언어학자    - improve 향상시키다
- electricity 전기    - experiment 실험

**O2** 다음 괄호 안에서 어법에 맞는 표현으로 가장 적절한 것을 고르시오.

> Chuseok is coming. My grandparents and some relatives live in Busan, so every Chuseok we go to Busan. Last year it took us about ten hours to drive back home. It was not easy **A**(for us / of us) to stay in a car for ten hours! I asked my parents **B**(to take / take) the KTX train to Busan this time. We went to Seoul Station and saw a lot of people **C**(to wait / waiting) in line to buy train tickets. We got in line and finally bought some tickets to Busan. We will have a comfortable journey this time.

- relative 친척    - wait in line 줄을 서서 기다리다

| | A | B | C |
|---|---|---|---|
| ① | for us | – take | – to wait |
| ② | for us | – take | – waiting |
| ③ | for us | – to take | – waiting |
| ④ | of us | – to take | – waiting |
| ⑤ | of us | – take | – to wait |

**O1** 다음 그림을 보고 빈칸에 알맞은 말을 쓰시오.

1)
I saw her _____ a book.

2)
I heard him _____.

3)
I made the baby _____.

**O2** 다음 우리말을 읽고 빈칸에 알맞은 말을 쓰시오.

앤(Ann)은 나에게 숙제를 도와달라고 청했다. 그녀는 내가 자기 집으로 오기를 원했다. 나는 그녀의 집으로 갔다. 나는 그녀의 방에서 그녀가 자고 있는 것을 보았다. 나는 그녀를 깨운 다음 우리는 함께 그녀의 숙제를 했다.

Ann asked me _____ _____ _____ _____ her homework. She _____ _____ _____ _____ to her house. I went to her house. I _____ _____ _____ in her room. I _____ _____ _____ and then we did her homework together.

- help A with B   A가 B하는 것을 도와주다

# Chapter 08

동명사

▶ 소 귀에 경 읽기

# 22 동명사의 역할

## A 주어 역할

'~하는 것은/이'로 해석한다.

**ex** • Swimming is good for your health.
• Studying English grammar is not easy.
• Climbing Mt. Everest is difficult.

## B 목적어 역할

'~하는 것을'로 해석한다.

### 1 동사의 목적어

**ex** • She finished baking his birthday cake.
• We enjoy talking on the phone.

### 2 전치사의 목적어

**ex** • I am interested in playing the guitar.
• They attacked without warning.

## C 보어 역할

'~하는 것이다'로 해석한다.

**ex** • His job is taking pictures.
• His hobby is playing tennis.

⊕ 동명사의 부정 : 동명사 앞에 **not, never**를 사용한다.

**ex** • Not telling a lie is important.

01 주어진 단어를 알맞은 형태로 바꾸어 빈칸에 쓰시오.

1) Thank you for _____ us. (invite)

2) He gave up _____. (cook)

3) Her job is _____ cars. (sell)

02 다음 문장의 **틀린** 부분에 밑줄을 긋고 바르게 고쳐 쓰시오.

1) He enjoyed meet her.                  (→ _____ )

2) She is good at speak English.          (→ _____ )

3) Talk to foreigners is interesting.      (→ _____ )

2) be good at
   ~을 잘하다

03 다음 문장을 우리말로 해석하시오.

1) Listening to music is relaxing.

→ _____

2) Her job is taking care of kids.

→ _____

3) He worried about failing the test.

→ _____

1) relaxing
   긴장을 풀어주는

04 우리말과 일치하도록 빈칸에 알맞은 말을 쓰시오.

1) 말을 타는 것은 흥미롭다.

→ _____ _____ _____ is interesting.

2) 그 목수들은 집 짓는 것을 끝냈다.

→ Those carpenters finished _____ a _____.

3) 그녀의 취미는 피아노를 치는 것이다.

→ Her hobby is _____ _____ _____.

2) carpenter 목수

# to부정사와 동명사

## A 동명사만을 목적어로 하는 동사

enjoy/finish/mind/give up/avoid + 동명사

ex
- We finished cleaning our room.
- She enjoys meeting new people.

## B to부정사만을 목적어로 하는 동사

decide, plan, promise, want, wish, hope, expect + to부정사

ex
- He decided to study in Canada.
- We hope to see him again.

## C 동명사와 to부정사를 목적어로 하는 동사

### 1 의미의 차이가 없는 경우

begin, start, love, like, hate + to부정사/동명사

ex
- She started to talk to him.
- She started talking to him.

### 2 의미가 달라지는 경우

remember, forget, stop, try + to부정사/동명사

ex
- She remembered to send the letter. (편지 보내야 하는 것을 기억함)
- She remembered sending the letter. (편지 보낸 것을 기억함)

- He forgot to call his parents. (전화해야 하는 것을 잊음)
- He forgot calling his parents. (전화한 것을 잊음)

- We stopped to talk. (말하기 위해 멈춤)
- We stopped talking. (말하는 것을 멈춤)

- I tried to call her. (전화하려고 노력함)
- I tried calling her. (시험 삼아 전화함)

정답 및 해설 p.14

**01** 주어진 단어를 알맞은 형태로 바꾸어 빈칸에 쓰시오.

1) She avoided _____ in the sea. (swim)

2) He promised _____ his word. (keep)

3) The baby began _____. (cry)

1) avoid  피하다

2) keep one's word
   약속을 지키다

**02** 빈칸에 들어갈 알맞은 말을 쓰시오.

1) I didn't send the letter. I forgot _____ it.

2) She talked to him yesterday.
   She remembers _____ to him.

3) Dad doesn't smoke anymore.
   Dad stopped _____.

**03** 다음 문장을 우리말로 해석하시오.

1) She stopped eating hamburgers.

   → _____

2) She stopped to eat hamburgers.

   → _____

3) I won't forget meeting him.

   → _____

4) I won't forget to meet him.

   → _____

**04** 다음 우리말을 영작하시오.

2) textbook  교과서

1) 그녀는 그녀의 자동차 열쇠를 찾으려고 애썼다.

   → _____

2) 그는 그 교과서 샀던 것을 기억한다.

   → _____

# 내신 족집게 **문제**

[01-02] 주어진 단어를 알맞은 형태로 바꾸어 빈칸에 쓰시오.

**01**  Do you mind _____ there alone?
　　　　　　　　　　　　　　　(go)

**02**  She planned _____ a birthday party.
　　　　　　　　　　　　　　　(have)

[03-05] 빈칸에 들어갈 수 <u>없는</u> 것을 고르시오.

**03**  He _____ to invent a time machine.

① wanted　　② hoped　　③ wished
④ gave up　　⑤ decided

**04**  She _____ talking to him.

① enjoys　　② likes　　③ minds
④ expects　　⑤ avoids

**05**  I _____ playing the piano with my friend, Jane.

① liked　　② hated　　③ wanted
④ loved　　⑤ started

**06**  주어진 단어를 알맞은 형태로 바꾸어 빈칸에 쓰시오.

A: I am so hungry.

B: How about _____ lunch early? (eat)

**07**  빈칸에 들어갈 알맞은 것을 고르시오.

_____ an English novel is interesting.

① Write　　② Wrote　　③ Written
④ To writing　　⑤ Writing

[08-10] 우리말과 일치하도록 빈칸에 알맞은 말을 쓰시오.

**08**  그는 물을 마시기 위해 멈췄다.

→ He stopped _____ water.

**09**  그는 그녀에게 그 책을 빌려 주었던 것을 기억한다.

→ He remembers _____ her the book.

**10**  나는 새 교과서를 사야 하는 것을 잊었다.

→ I forgot _____ a new textbook.

**11**  빈칸에 알맞은 단어를 순서대로 바르게 짝지은 것을 고르시오.

• They finished _____ the dishes.
• She promised _____ to my birthday party.

① washing – coming
② washing – to come
③ wash – come
④ to wash – coming
⑤ to wash – to come

**12**  빈칸에 공통으로 들어갈 sing의 알맞은 형태를 쓰시오.

• She stopped _____.
• She is good at _____.

13 두 문장의 뜻이 같도록 빈칸에 알맞은 말을 쓰시오.

She started to study English grammar every day.

= She started _____ English grammar every day.

14 우리말과 일치하도록 빈칸에 알맞은 말을 쓰시오.

그는 그 여행 가방을 열려고 애썼다.

→ He tried _____ _____ the suitcase.

[15-16] 보기의 밑줄 친 부분과 쓰임이 같은 것을 고르시오.

15 보기 Her favorite hobby is building figures with lego bricks.

① The girl is playing the piano.
② We are having lunch.
③ His job is taking pictures.
④ The old man is painting the door.
⑤ Those children are going to the park.

16 보기 The baby boy was crying. His mom gave him something to eat. Then he stopped crying.

① Reading comics is fun.
② Her job is selling books.
③ We are doing our homework.
④ He finished fixing his bike.
⑤ Saving money is not easy.

17 다음 중 어법상 틀린 문장을 고르시오.

① They are interested in joining the club.
② He wants to stay at home.
③ I hate playing the violin.
④ She enjoys to sing.
⑤ He planned to learn French.

18 밑줄 친 부분의 역할이 나머지와 다른 것을 고르시오.

① She likes playing the guitar.
② She finished making lunch.
③ She left without saying anything.
④ Traveling is interesting.
⑤ He tried dancing.

19 다음 중 올바른 문장을 고르시오.

① I enjoy to read English novels.
② Remember meeting me at 5 tomorrow.
③ The baby began to cry.
④ He gave up smoke.
⑤ She expected seeing her friends there.

20 두 문장의 뜻이 같지 않은 것을 고르시오.

① She began to play the piano.
= She began playing the piano.
② He hates to talk to her.
= He hates talking to her.
③ I love to go to the concert.
= I love going to the concert.
④ They started to laugh.
= They started laughing.
⑤ We stopped cleaning the classroom.
= We stopped to clean the classroom.

정답 및 해설 p.15

O1 다음 글의 밑줄 친 부분 중 어법상 틀린 것을 고르시오.

> Paul was good at ① baking chocolate cakes, so he made chocolate cakes for his family and friends. He started ② working at a bakery when he was in high school. He hoped ③ opening a bakery someday. When he was 28, he opened his own bakery. He worked almost all day to find a new recipe for chocolate cake. ④ Making perfect and delicious chocolate cakes was not easy but he didn't give up ⑤ making an effort. After failing a hundred times, he finally made a delicious chocolate cake. The cake, called Paul's cake, is sold all over the world. Now, he is a millionaire baker!

- recipe 요리법    - delicious 맛있는
- millionaire 백만장자

O2 다음 괄호 안에서 어법에 맞는 표현으로 가장 적절한 것을 고르시오.

> Jane forgot Ⓐ(to bring / bringing) her new textbook to school. Yesterday she went to a bookstore to buy it. Last night she talked to her friends about the book on the phone. They stopped Ⓑ(to talk / talking) around 10. Then she remembered Ⓒ(to put / putting) the book on the desk. When she opened her bag at school, the textbook was not there. Probably the book was still on the desk in her room.

|   | Ⓐ |   | Ⓑ |   | Ⓒ |
|---|---|---|---|---|---|
| ① | to bring | – | to talk | – | to put |
| ② | to bring | – | talking | – | putting |
| ③ | to bring | – | to talk | – | putting |
| ④ | bringing | – | talking | – | to put |
| ⑤ | bringing | – | to talk | – | putting |

O1 자연스러운 대화가 되도록 주어진 단어를 이용하여 빈칸에 알맞은 말을 쓰시오.

Ann : I enjoy _____ the piano. (play)

Jane : I wasn't good at music.

   I stopped _____ the violin when I was 13. (play)

Ann : Then, what are you interested in?

Jane : I am interested in _____ a foreign language. (learn)

O2 다음 우리말을 읽고 바르게 영작하시오.

오늘 할 일이 많았다. 나는 존(John)에게 전화하려고 애썼다. 나는 제인(Jane)에게 이메일 하는 것을 잊었다. 나는 데이비드(David)와 함께 이야기했던 것을 기억한다. 나는 숙제하는 것을 끝냈다.

There were many things to do today.

_____

_____

_____

Chapter 09

분사

## Chapter 미리보기

| 현재분사 | 과거분사 |
|---|---|
| 동사원형 + -ing | 동사원형 + -ed 또는 불규칙 변화 |
| ~하고 있는 → 진행, 능동의 의미<br>falling leaves (떨어지고 있는 잎들) | ~된, ~하여진 → 완료, 수동의 의미<br>fallen leaves (떨어진 잎들) |
| 주어와 보어의 능동 관계<br>The game was exciting. (game이 흥분을 일으킴) | 주어와 보어의 수동 관계<br>We were excited. (We가 흥분이 됨) |

**A rolling stone gathers no moss.** 구르는 돌에는 이끼가 끼지 않는다.

▶ 부지런하고 꾸준히 노력하는 사람은 정체되지 않고 계속 발전한다.

# Unit 24 현재분사와 과거분사

## A 현재분사와 과거분사의 의미

현재분사는 〈동사원형 + -ing〉의 형태이며, 진행형에서 사용된다.
과거분사는 〈동사원형 + -ed〉의 형태이며, 완료시제와 수동태에서 사용된다.

ex
- I am playing soccer.
- He has lived in Seoul for 4 years.
- The chair is made of wood.

## B 현재분사와 과거분사의 쓰임

1  **명사 수식** : 현재분사는 '～하고 있는'으로 해석하며, 능동적 진행의 의미를 가지고 있다.
　　　　　 과거분사는 '～된, ～하여진'으로 해석하며, 수동적 완료의 의미를 가지고 있다.

ex
- singing boys → 노래하는 소년들
- the girl dancing on the stage → 무대에서 춤추는 소녀
- a car made in Korea → 한국에서 만든 차
- a broken vase → 깨어진 꽃병

2  **주격 보어** : 〈주어 + 동사 + 보어〉 구문에서 보어 자리에 분사가 올 수 있다.
　　　　　 현재분사는 주어와 보어가 능동 관계이며, 과거분사는 수동 관계이다.

ex
- The boy came running. → boy가 running하기 때문에 현재분사를 쓴다.
- People felt excited. → people이 흥미를 느끼게 되었기 때문에 과거분사를 쓴다.

**Tips**
- 지각동사 뒤의 목적격 보어로 동사원형이 올 수도 있다.

3  지각동사(see, watch, hear, feel 등) 다음의 목적격 보어 자리에는 현재분사가 올 수 있다.

ex
- I saw my son skating.
- He heard her playing the flute.

### ⊕ 동명사와 현재분사의 비교

| 동명사 | 현재분사 |
|---|---|
| 동명사 + 명사(용도, 목적을 나타냄) | 현재분사 + 명사(진행중인 동작을 나타냄) |
| a sleeping bag = a bag for sleeping(침낭) | a sleeping princess(잠자고 있는 공주) |

# Grammar Check-Up

**O1** 다음 중 알맞은 것을 고르시오.

1) They have   met | meeting   my mother once.

2) I saw a   boring | bored   movie yesterday.

3) She watched him   playing | played   tennis.

**O2** 우리말과 일치하도록 주어진 말을 알맞은 형태로 바꾸어 빈칸에 쓰시오.

1) 나는 어제 중고차를 샀다.

→ I bought a _____ car yesterday. (use)

2) 나는 길에서 옆집에 사는 사람을 만났다.

→ I met the man _____ next door on the street. (live)

3) 깨어진 접시는 버리세요.

→ Please throw away the _____ plate. (break)

3) throw away 버리다

**O3** 밑줄 친 부분에 주의하여 다음 문장을 우리말로 해석하시오.

1) Minyeong always reads books written in English.

→ _____

2) My father needs a walking stick when he goes out.

→ _____

3) The people walking along the river look happy.

→ _____

**O4** 다음 우리말을 영작하시오.

1) 너 지루해 보인다.

→ _____

2) 수학은 재미있는 과목이다.

→ _____

# Unit 25 분사구문

**분사구문**이란 부사절을 분사가 있는 문장으로 표현하는 것을 말한다.
즉, 〈접속사 + 주어 + 동사〉를 〈동사원형 + -ing〉의 형태로 바꾸는 것이다.

## A 분사구문을 만드는 방법

**Tips**
• 분사구문의 부정은 〈not + 분사〉가 된다.
• 부사절이 진행형일 때 Being은 생략한다.

① 접속사를 생략한다.
② (주절과 종속절의 주어가 같을 때) 주어를 삭제한다.
③ 동사원형에 -ing를 붙인다.

**ex** • As she loved him, she married him.
→ Loving him, she married him.
• If you don't go to bed now, you will get up late.
→ Not going to bed now, you will get up late.
• While she was reading books, she ate some cookies.
→ Reading books, she ate some cookies.

## B 분사구문의 의미

**1 때** : when (~할 때), while (~동안에)

**2 이유** : because, as (~때문에)

**3 조건** : if (만약 ~라면)

**4 양보** : though, although (비록 ~이지만)

**5 동시동작** : as (~하면서)

**ex** • Living in Korea, she worked as a teacher.
→ When she lived in Korea, she worked as a teacher.
• Being a foreigner, she needs a visa.
→ As she is a foreigner, she needs a visa.
• Having a cold, I went out.
→ Though I had a cold, I went out.

정답 및 해설 p.15

○1 다음 문장을 분사구문으로 바꿀 때 빈칸에 알맞은 말을 쓰시오.

1) Though I was tired, I couldn't sleep.

→ _____ _____, I couldn't sleep.

2) As she didn't wear a coat, she was very cold.

→ _____ _____ _____

_____, she was very cold.

○2 밑줄 친 부분에 주의하여 다음 문장을 우리말로 해석하시오.

1) Not knowing his email address, I can't email him.

→ _____

2) Watching a movie, I fell asleep.

→ _____

○3 두 문장의 뜻이 같도록 빈칸에 알맞은 말을 쓰시오.

1) Being kind and pretty, she is loved by everyone.

= _____ _____ is kind and pretty, she is loved

by everyone.

2) Being ill yesterday, he went to school.

= _____ _____ _____ ill yesterday,

he went to school.

2) ill 아픈

○4 우리말과 일치하도록 빈칸에 알맞은 말을 쓰시오.

1) 나는 아침을 먹지 않았기 때문에 배가 몹시 고팠다.

→ Because I _____ _____ _____, I was very hungry.

→ _____ _____ _____, I was very hungry.

2) 그녀는 샤워하면서 노래를 부른다.

→ As she _____ _____ _____, she sings a song.

→ _____ _____ _____, she sings a song.

2) take a shower
샤워하다

[01 - 02] 빈칸에 들어갈 알맞은 것을 고르시오.

**01**　Cameras _____ in Korea are very good.

① making　　② made　　③ to make
④ is making　　⑤ is made

**02**　The girl _____ flowers there is my sister.

① watered　　　　② water
③ watering　　　　④ to watering
⑤ is watering

**03**　빈칸에 알맞은 단어를 순서대로 바르게 짝지은 것을 고르시오.

· The baseball game was _____.
· We were _____ about getting free tickets.

① exciting – excited　　② exciting – exciting
③ excited – excited　　④ excited – exciting
⑤ excitingly – excited

[04 - 05] 우리말과 일치하도록 빈칸에 알맞은 것을 고르시오.

**04**　깨진 꽃병을 버리세요.
　　→ Please throw away the _____ vase.

① broken　　② breaking　　③ broke
④ breaked　　⑤ break

**05**　우리는 펄럭이는 깃발을 볼 수 있다.
　　→ We can see _____ flags.

① to fly　　② flown　　③ flew
④ flied　　⑤ flying

[06 - 07] 두 문장의 뜻이 같도록 빈칸에 들어갈 알맞은 것을 고르시오.

**06**　While he was taking a walk, he found 10,000 won.
　　= _____ a walk, he found 10,000 won.

① He taking　　② Taking　　③ Taken
④ To take　　⑤ He taken

**07**　As I don't speak English, I can't understand what he says.
　　= _____ English, I can't understand what he says.

① Don't speaking　　② Not speaking
③ Don't speak　　④ Not speak
⑤ Not being speaking

**08**　빈칸에 공통으로 들어갈 알맞은 것을 고르시오.

· My sister is _____ a bicycle.
· I saw children _____ bicycles.

① to ride　　② ride　　③ rode
④ ridden　　⑤ riding

**09**　빈칸에 들어갈 수 <u>없는</u> 것을 고르시오.

The book is very _____.

① shocking　　② boring　　③ bored
④ interesting　　⑤ easy

**10**　다음 문장을 분사구문으로 바꿀 때 빈칸에 알맞은 말을 쓰시오.

As she had no time, she took a taxi.
　　→ _____ no time, she took a taxi.

11  우리말과 일치하도록 빈칸에 공통으로 들어갈 알맞은 말을 쓰시오.

· 흡연실이 어디입니까?
→ Where is the _____ room?
· 저기 담배 피우는 남자를 보시오.
→ Look at the _____ man.

12  밑줄 친 부분의 쓰임이 나머지와 <u>다른</u> 것을 고르시오.

① Look at the flying birds.
② My father is looking for a sleeping bag.
③ A prince kissed the sleeping princess.
④ The girls dancing on the stage are very pretty.
⑤ Here is surprising news.

13  두 문장의 뜻이 같도록 빈칸에 알맞은 말을 쓰시오.

Working all day long, I was not tired.
= _____ I worked all day long, I was not tired.

14  두 문장의 뜻이 같지 <u>않은</u> 것을 고르시오.

① The boy who is playing with Harry is John.
= The boy playing with Harry is John.
② The people invited to the party have to come early.
= The people who are invited to the party have to come early.
③ Because I was on vacation, I visited many countries.
= Being on vacation, I visited many countries.
④ Though she likes to listen to music, she doesn't sing well.
= Liking to listen to music, she doesn't sing well.
⑤ If it is hot tomorrow, we will go swimming.
= Being hot tomorrow, we will go swimming.

[15-16] 밑줄 친 부분이 어법상 <u>틀린</u> 것을 고르시오.

15  ① He has written a novel.
② He is writing a novel.
③ The man writing the novel is my father.
④ The novel writing in English is not easy.
⑤ The novel was written by my father.

16  ① There are a lot of fallen leaves on the street.
② Barking dogs never bite.
③ We have just found the stolen car.
④ I felt somebody touched my back.
⑤ He was carried out of the car.

[17-18] 우리말과 일치하도록 빈칸에 알맞은 말을 쓰시오.

17  나는 그가 피아노 치는 것을 들었다.
→ I heard him _____ _____ _____.

18  강에서 수영하고 있는 아이들이 몇 명 있다.
→ There are some children _____ in the river.

[19-20] 우리말과 일치하도록 주어진 단어를 알맞게 배열하시오.

19  저기 사진을 찍고 있는 외국인들을 보아라.
(taking, over there, pictures, foreigners, look at, the)
→ _____

20  내가 영국에 도착했을 때 너에게 전화할 것이다.
(call, I, will, arriving, England, in, you)
→ _____

정답 및 해설 p.16

○1 다음 빈칸에 들어갈 말로 가장 적절한 것을 고르시오.

> The sandwich is one of the most popular snacks in the world. Where does the word 'sandwich' come from? The word 'sandwich' was born in London in 1792. The Earl of Sandwich loved gambling. He couldn't stop gambling even to eat. He ordered a servant to put roast-beef between two slices of bread. He continued to gamble, **A**_____ this food. We now call this food a sandwich, which was **B**_____ after the Earl of Sandwich.

- earl 백작  - roast-beef 구운 쇠고기  - continue 계속하다
- gamble 도박을 하다

|  | A | B |  | A | B |
|---|---|---|---|---|---|
| ① | ate | – named | ② | eaten | – named |
| ③ | eating | – name | ④ | eating | – naming |
| ⑤ | eating | – named |  |  |  |

○2 다음 빈칸에 들어갈 말로 가장 적절한 것을 고르시오.

> Before Karen went **A**_____ last Sunday morning, she made some cookies. She told her brother Brian not to eat any of them. He and his friend Tim were playing computer games. However, after a while they got **B**_____. They went into the kitchen and saw the cookies. Each of them stole two. They ate them with a glass of milk and went out.

- after a while 잠시 후에  - steal 훔치다

|  | A | B |  | A | B |
|---|---|---|---|---|---|
| ① | to shop | – boring | ② | shopping | – bored |
| ③ | shopping | – excited | ④ | shopping | – boring |
| ⑤ | to shop | – exciting |  |  |  |

○1 다음 그림을 보고 주어진 단어를 이용하여 빈칸에 알맞은 말을 쓰시오.

| 보기 | The baby crying in the room is my sister. |
|---|---|
|  | (cry) |

1) The girl _____ the violin looks pretty.
   (play)

2) Look at the leaves _____ on the bench.
   (fall)

○2 다음 우리말을 읽고 바르게 영작하시오.

나는 오늘 아침 늦게 일어났다. 나는 어머니께서 내 이름을 부르시는 것을 들었지만 일어날 수 없었다. 나는 아버지께서 내 방으로 들어오시는 것을 보았다. 나는 침대에서 벌떡 일어났다.

I got up late this morning.

_____

_____

_____

I jumped out of my bed.

Chapter 10

수동태

## Chapter 미리보기

| | 능동태(주어가 동작을 행함) | 수동태(주어가 동작을 받음) |
|---|---|---|
| 현재 | I write a letter. | A letter is written by me. |
| 과거 | I wrote a letter. | A letter was written by me. |
| 미래 | I will write a letter. | A letter will be written by me. |

▶ 시작이 반이다.

# 26 능동태와 수동태의 의미와 형태

Tips
• '태'는 주어와 동사와의 관계를 말한다.

## A 능동태와 수동태

능동태는 주어가 동사의 동작을 행하는 것을 말한다.
수동태는 주어가 동사의 동작을 받거나 당하는 것을 의미한다.

ex • Many people love the actor. (능동태 → many people이 사랑을 한다.)
   • The actor is loved by many people. (수동태 → the actor가 사랑을 받는다.)

## B 수동태 만드는 방법

① 능동태의 목적어를 수동태의 주어 자리에 놓는다.
② 능동태의 시제와 인칭을 고려하여 동사를 〈be동사 + 과거분사〉로 한다.
③ 능동태의 주어를 수동태의 〈by + 목적격〉으로 만든다.

ex • Thomas Edison      invented      the light bulb.

   → The light bulb was invented by Thomas Edison.

## C 수동태의 시제

1  현재시제 : am/are/is + 과거분사

   ex • Sue cleans the room.
      → The room is cleaned by Sue.

2  과거시제 : was/were + 과거분사

   ex • He painted the wall.
      → The wall was painted by him.

3  미래시제 : will be + 과거분사

   ex • They will invite you to a party.
      → You will be invited to a party by them.

정답 및 해설 p.16

○1 다음 중 알맞은 것을 고르시오.

1) The car   washes | is washed   by her every day.

2) She   invited | was invited   her boyfriend to a party.

3) This house   built | was built   by my father.


○2 다음 문장을 수동태로 바꿀 때 빈칸에 들어갈 알맞은 말을 쓰시오.

1) I took this picture.

→ This picture _____ _____ _____ _____.

2) Many people use the Internet.

→ The Internet _____ _____ _____ _____

_____.

3) She will paint the wall.

→ The wall _____ _____ _____ _____

_____.


○3 다음 문장을 우리말로 해석하시오.

1) *Hamlet* was written by Shakespeare.

→ _____

2) This road isn't used by many people.

→ _____

3) I will be visited by my friends tomorrow.

→ _____


○4 다음 우리말을 영작하시오.

1) 브라이언은 많은 팬들의 사랑을 받는다.

→ Brian _____.

2) 한글은 세종대왕(King Sejong)이 창제하셨다.

→ Hangeul _____.

2) create
창제하다, 만들다

# 27 여러 가지 수동태

### A 4형식 문장의 수동태

4형식은 〈주어 + 동사 + 간접목적어 + 직접목적어〉로 이루어진 문장이며, 목적어가 두 개이므로 수동태를 두 개 만들 수 있다. 단, write, buy, make, send 등이 쓰인 문장은 직접목적어로만 수동태를 만들 수 있다.

**ex** • He teaches us math.
→ We are taught math by him.
→ Math is taught to us by him.

• He made her a beautiful dress.
→ A beautiful dress was made for her by him.
→ She was made a beautiful dress by him. (×)

⊕ 직접목적어로 수동태 문장을 만들 때 간접목적어 앞에 쓰는 전치사

**ex** • give, send, write, show → to
• buy, make → for
• ask → of

### B 5형식 문장의 수동태

5형식은 〈주어 + 동사 + 목적어 + 목적격 보어〉로 이루어진 문장이며, 목적어가 수동태 문장의 주어가 된다.

**ex** • We call it popcorn.
→ It is called popcorn (by us).

### C 조동사가 있는 문장의 수동태

조동사가 있는 문장의 수동태는 〈조동사 + be + 과거분사〉가 된다.

**ex** • You should clean the room.
→ The room should be cleaned by you.

**Tips**
• run over 치다
• take care of 돌보다
• bring up 키우다
• throw away 버리다

### D 동사구의 수동태

**ex** • They laughed at him.
→ He was laughed at by them.

# Grammar Check-Up

정답 및 해설 p.16

**01** 다음 중 알맞은 것을 고르시오.

1) The girl   is called | called   Karen by her friends.

2) The music   can be heard | can hear | can is heard   from far away.

3) He   was laughed by | was laughed at by   his classmates.

2) far away 멀리서

**02** 다음 문장을 수동태로 바꿀 때 빈칸에 들어갈 알맞은 말을 쓰시오.

1) The man asked her a lot of questions.

→ A lot of questions _____ _____ _____

_____ by the man.

2) Brian gave me a present.

→ I _____ _____ _____ _____ by Brian.

3) Karen should take care of her sister.

→ Her sister _____ _____ _____ _____

_____ by Karen.

**03** 다음 문장을 우리말로 해석하시오.

1) A cat was run over by a truck.

→ _____

2) We were taught Taekwondo by him.

→ _____

3) The girl is called a little princess by her parents.

→ _____

**04** 다음 우리말을 영작하시오.

1) 이 강아지는 누군가에 의해 버려졌다.

→ This puppy _____ .

2) 이 문장은 그 학생들에 의해 반드시 기억되어야 한다.

→ This sentence _____ .

1) throw away 버리다
2) sentence 문장

Unit 27 ☆ **97**

# Unit 28 주의해야 할 수동태

## A  <by + 목적격>의 생략

능동태의 주어가 일반적인 사람이거나 동작의 행위자가 불분명할 때 수동태 문장에서 〈by + 목적격〉은 생략할 수 있다.

**1  일반적인 사람일 때**

> ex ▸ • English is spoken in New Zealand (by people).
> • Thousands of cattle are raised here.

**2  행위자가 불분명할 때**

> ex ▸ • The building was built in 1960.
> • My father was killed in a war.
> • This dictionary is designed for children.
> • My jewel was stolen.

## B  by 이외의 다른 전치사를 쓰는 경우

| | |
|---|---|
| be interested in | ~에 흥미를 갖다 |
| be pleased with | ~에 기뻐하다 |
| be surprised at/by | ~에 놀라다 |
| be covered with | ~로 덮여있다 |
| be known to | ~에게 알려지다 |
| be satisfied with | ~에 만족하다 |
| be filled with | ~로 가득차다 |

> ex ▸ • I am interested in cooking.
> • My parents were pleased with my present.
> • I was surprised at you.
> • The roof of my house is covered with snow.
> • Korean dramas are known to many Asian people.
> • My mother was satisfied with my exam results.
> • The box is filled with candies.

# Grammar Check-Up

**01** 다음 중 알맞은 것을 고르시오.

1) English   speak | is spoken | is speaking   in New Zealand.

2) A famous designer   designed | was designed   our uniform.

3) Pablo Picasso is known   to | for   many people.

**02** 우리말과 일치하도록 빈칸에 알맞은 말을 쓰시오.

1) 이 차는 1980년대에 한국에서 만들어졌다.

→ This car _____ _____ in Korea in the 1980s.

2) 나는 사극에 흥미를 갖고 있다.

→ I am _____ _____ historical dramas.

3) 이 거리는 낙엽으로 덮여있다.

→ This street is _____ _____ fallen leaves.

2) historical drama 사극

**03** 다음 문장을 우리말로 해석하시오.

1) Yonsei University was founded in 1885.

→ _____

2) My bike was stolen last night.

→ _____

3) My mother was satisfied with my final exam results.

→ _____

1) found 설립하다

2) steal (– stole – stolen) 훔치다

**04** 다음 우리말을 영작하시오.

1) 나는 1990년에 태어났다.

→ _____

2) 그들은 그녀의 성공에 기뻐했다.

→ _____

2) success 성공

# 내신 족집게 문제

**01** 빈칸에 들어갈 수 <u>없는</u> 것을 고르시오.

This pizza was made by _____.

① them    ② me    ③ her
④ he    ⑤ my mother

**[02-05]** 빈칸에 들어갈 알맞은 것을 고르시오.

**02** The house _____ by Sumi yesterday.

① is cleaned    ② cleans    ③ was cleaned
④ cleaned    ⑤ was cleaning

**03** The problem can _____ by many students.

① solve    ② is solved    ③ be solving
④ be solved    ⑤ solves

**04** Tommy was not _____ any presents by his parents on Christmas day.

① gave    ② gives    ③ giving
④ gived    ⑤ given

**05** The roof of my house is covered _____ snow.

① with    ② at    ③ on
④ of    ⑤ to

**06** 빈칸에 공통으로 들어갈 알맞은 것을 고르시오.

• Her school bag is filled _____ comic books.
• She was satisfied _____ my answer.

① with    ② by    ③ in
④ of    ⑤ to

**[07-09]** 두 문장의 뜻이 같도록 빈칸에 알맞은 말을 쓰시오.

**07** Shakespeare wrote *King Lear*.

→ *King Lear* _____ _____

_____ _____.

**08** You should throw away the old books.

→ The old books _____ _____

_____ _____ by you.

**09** She found the dog last night.

= _____ _____ _____

_____ _____ _____ last night.

**10** 두 문장의 뜻이 같도록 빈칸에 알맞은 단어를 순서대로 바르게 짝지은 것을 고르시오.

He _____ the poor boy.
= The poor boy _____ by him.

① helps – is helping    ② helps – is helped
③ is helping – help    ④ is helped – helped
⑤ is helped – is helped

**[11-12]** 빈칸에 알맞은 단어를 순서대로 바르게 짝지은 것을 고르시오.

**11**
• *Sunflower* was painted _____ Gogh.
• This song is known _____ many people.

① by – to    ② with – for    ③ of – by
④ by – for    ⑤ by – as

12
- The house _____ in 1930.
- The house _____ next year.

① is built – is built
② built – will build
③ was building – will be building
④ was built – will be built
⑤ built – built

13 다음 문장을 수동태로 바르게 바꾼 것을 고르시오.

  He made her the dress.

① He was made her the dress.
② She was made the dress by him.
③ The dress was made to her by him.
④ The dress was made for her by him.
⑤ The dress was made by her.

14 밑줄 친 부분이 어법상 틀린 것을 고르시오.
① The book was written in Spanish.
② Cheese is made from milk.
③ He took me to Dongdaemoon market yesterday.
④ This dictionary designed for children.
⑤ The teacher is respected by them.

15 다음 중 올바른 문장을 고르시오.
① The old people should be help by someone.
② He is call Brian.
③ She was pleased with the gift.
④ The baby was taken care of a nurse.
⑤ The window was broken by he.

16 빈칸에 들어갈 단어가 나머지와 다른 것을 고르시오.
① The work was finished _____ my sister.
② The telephone was invented _____ Bell.
③ The singer is loved _____ a lot of fans.
④ This poem was written _____ Frost.
⑤ Both French and English are spoken _____ Canada.

17 두 문장의 뜻이 같도록 빈칸에 알맞은 말을 쓰시오.

  This car was used by my father.
  = My father _____ this car.

18 다음 문장의 의미가 나머지와 다른 것을 고르시오.
① She taught me math.
② She taught math to me.
③ I was taught math by her.
④ Math was taught to me by her.
⑤ I taught her math.

[19-20] 우리말과 일치하도록 주어진 단어를 알맞게 배열하시오.

19 그는 학급 친구들에게 비웃음을 받았다.
(classmates, was, he, laughed, by, at, his)
→ _____

20 그 소년은 병원으로 보내졌다.
(the, taken, hospital, to, was, the, boy)
→ _____

정답 및 해설 pp.17-18

**01** 다음 글의 밑줄 친 부분 중 어법상 <u>틀린</u> 것을 고르시오.

> Koalas are only ① found in Australia. Early settlers ② were called them Native Bears because they ③ looked like bears. However, they are very different from bears. They have a pouch. 'Koala' is an aboriginal word meaning 'no drink.' It is a good name. They don't drink water. They get all the water that they need from eucalyptus leaves. Until the late 1920's, they ④ were hunted for their skin. However, they ⑤ are now protected and loved as Australia's most famous animal.

- be different from ~와 다르다
- aboriginal 원주민의
- protect 보호하다

**02** 다음 괄호 안에서 어법에 맞는 표현으로 가장 적절한 것을 고르시오.

> The Korean language Ⓐ(was invented / invented) by King Sejong the Great in 1443. It was first called Huminjeongeum. Since the beginning of the 20th century, it has been called Hanguel. Until 1442, Koreans Ⓑ(used / were used) Chinese letters for their writing system. However, Chinese was very different from the language that Koreans used. It was very hard to learn and use. King Sejong the Great loved his people very much, so he decided Ⓒ(to create / creating) Hanguel.

- invent 발명하다
- century 세기

| Ⓐ | | Ⓑ | | Ⓒ |
|---|---|---|---|---|
| ① was invented | – | were used | – | to create |
| ② was invented | – | used | – | creating |
| ③ was invented | – | used | – | to create |
| ④ invented | – | were used | – | to create |
| ⑤ invented | – | used | – | to create |

**01** 다음 주어진 단어를 이용하여 보기처럼 빈칸에 알맞은 말을 쓰시오.

> Yi Sunsin    a turtle ship    make    1591
> Columbus    America    discover    1492

> 보기   Yi Sunsin made a turtle ship in 1591.
> = A turtle ship was made by Yi Sunsin in 1591.

Columbus _____ _____ _____

_____ .

= America _____ _____ _____

_____ _____ _____ .

**02** 다음 우리말을 읽고 바르게 영작하시오.

우리는 어제 오래된 성을 방문했다. 그 성은 1800년에 지어졌다. 벽과 문은 검은 색으로 칠해져 있었다. 지붕은 까마귀로 덮여있었다. 우리는 무서웠다.

We visited an old castle yesterday.

_____

_____

_____

_____

- crow 까마귀
- scared 무서워하는

# Chapter 11

## Chapter 미리보기

| 시간을 나타내는 접속사 | when, as, while, until, before, after |
|---|---|
| 이유, 결과를 나타내는 접속사 | as, since, because, so, so ~ that 주어 can/can't |
| 조건, 양보를 나타내는 접속사 | if, unless, though, although, even though |
| 명사절을 이끄는 접속사 | that, if, whether |
| 명령문 + and | ~해라, 그러면 …할 것이다 |
| 명령문 + or | ~해라, 그렇지 않으면 …할 것이다 |
| 상관접속사 | both A and B, either A or B, neither A nor B<br>not only A but also B = B as well as A |

When the cat is away, the mice will play. 고양이가 없으면 쥐가 설친다.

▶ 호랑이가 없는 골에 토끼가 왕 노릇한다.

# 29 시간을 나타내는 접속사

**Tips**
- when은 의문사로도 쓰인다.
- 접속사 as는 두 가지 일이 동시에 일어나는 경우에 주로 사용한다.

## A when

〜할 때

**ex**
- I went to Canada when I was nine years old.
  = When I was nine years old, I went to Canada.

## B as

〜할 때

**ex**
- As we entered the restaurant, we saw Jane.

## C while

〜하는 동안

**ex**
- We met David while we were walking along the beach.

## D before/after

〜전에/〜후에

**ex**
- Before they had lunch, they washed their hands.
- After they washed their hands, they had lunch.

⊕ before, after, until이 전치사로 사용되면 뒤에 명사(구)가 온다.

**ex**
- He played the piano before lunch. → 전치사로 사용

## E until

〜까지

**ex**
- I will study English until I go to bed.

⊕ 시간의 부사절에서는 현재시제가 미래시제를 대신한다.

**ex**
- When Dad finishes his work, he will come home. (○)
  When Dad will finish his work, he will come home. (×)
- He will wait for her until she comes. (○)
  He will wait for her until she will come. (×)

**01** 다음 중 알맞은 것을 고르시오.

1) As ¦ Until  I came into the room, the boy ran away.

2) She writes a diary  after ¦ before  she goes to bed.

3) He will watch TV when he  will get ¦ gets  home.

1) run away 도망가다

**02** 빈칸에 알맞은 접속사를 쓰시오.

1) 그녀는 방과 후에 그를 만날 수 있었다.

→ She could meet him _____ school.

2) 내가 숙제를 하는 동안 전기가 나갔다.

→ The electricity went out _____ I was doing my homework.

2) electricity 전기

**03** 다음 문장을 우리말로 해석하시오.

1) I turned off the computer before I went shopping.

→ _____

2) When she was eleven, she went to China.

→ _____

3) When did she go home?

→ _____

1) go shopping 쇼핑하러 가다

**04** 우리말과 일치하도록 빈칸에 알맞은 말을 쓰시오.

1) 데이비드(David)가 집에 간 후에 제인이 왔다.

→ Jane came _____ _____ _____

_____.

2) 그녀는 그가 사과할 때까지 그와 말하지 않을 것이다.

→ She won't speak to him _____ _____

_____ to her.

3) 그는 12살 때 축구 선수가 되었다.

→ He became a football player _____ _____

_____ twelve.

2) apologize 사과하다

# 30 이유, 결과를 나타내는 접속사

## A because

~때문에

ex ▸ • Because it was cold, she wore a coat and a pair of gloves.
  • She was late for school because she missed the school bus.

⊕ because of 다음에는 명사(구)가 온다.

ex ▸ • She stayed at home because of the weather.

## B as

~때문에

ex ▸ • As he likes her, he will invite her to his birthday party.
  • As we were hungry, we went to a restaurant.
  • As we were leaving the restaurant, we met our teacher. ('~할 때'의 뜻으로 쓰임)

## C since

~때문에

ex ▸ • He couldn't visit us since he was busy.
  • She can't open her car since she lost her car key.
  • I have lived here since I was nine. ('~이래로'의 뜻으로 쓰임)

## D so

그래서

ex ▸ • I was tired, so I went to bed early.
    = I went to bed early because I was tired.

## E so ~ that 주어 can/can't

너무 ~해서 …할 수 있다/없다

ex ▸ • She is so kind that she can help us.
    = She is kind enough to help us.
  • He is so small that he can't wear this.
    = He is too small to wear this.

# Grammar **Check-Up**

**01** 다음 중 알맞은 것을 고르시오.

1) She fell down  because of | because  the floor was slippery.

2) She couldn't go to school  because of | because  the snow.

3) He lost his favorite pet  because | so  he was sad.

*1) slippery 미끄러운*

**02** 두 문장의 뜻이 같도록 빈칸에 알맞은 말을 쓰시오.

1) He was so brave that he could catch the thief.

= He was _____ _____ to catch the thief.

2) He was so poor that he couldn't buy clothes.

= He was _____ _____ to buy clothes.

**03** 다음 문장을 우리말로 해석하시오.

1) As she was angry, she shouted at him.

→ _____

2) As Ann got off the bus, Paul hugged her.

→ _____

3) Since she was ill, she didn't go to school.

→ _____

*1) shout 소리치다*
*2) hug 껴안다*

**04** 우리말과 일치하도록 빈칸에 알맞은 말을 쓰시오.

1) 나는 배가 너무 고파서 무엇이든 먹을 수 있다.

→ I'm so _____ _____ I _____
_____ anything.

2) 그는 그것이 너무 어려워서 풀 수 없었다.

→ It was so _____ _____ he _____
_____ it.

3) 그는 너무 피곤해서 소파에서 잠이 들었다.

→ He was very tired, _____ _____
_____ _____ on the sofa.

*3) fall asleep 잠들다*

# 31 조건, 양보를 나타내는 접속사, that

## A if

만약 ~한다면

ex ▸ • If she finishes her homework earlier, she will go to the movies.
   • If it is sunny tomorrow, we will go to the beach.

⊕ if가 명사절에서는 '~인지 아닌지'의 뜻으로도 사용된다.

ex ▸ • We don't know if she likes him.
   = We don't know whether she likes him.

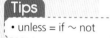

Tips
• unless = if ~ not

## B unless

만약 ~하지 않는다면

ex ▸ • I will go to your house unless you come to my house.
   = I will go to your house if you do not come to my house.
   • Ann will eat the cake unless you eat it.
   = Ann will eat the cake if you do not eat it.

⊕ 조건을 나타내는 부사절에서는 현재시제가 미래시제를 대신한다.

ex ▸ • If it is rainy tomorrow, I will stay at home. (○)
   • If it will be rainy tomorrow, I will stay at home. (×)

## C though, although, even though, even if

비록 ~일지라도

ex ▸ • Although he is young, he is wise.
   • Though she doesn't like spinach, she sometimes eats it.

## D that

접속사 that이 목적절을 이끌 경우 생략 가능하다.

ex ▸ • I know (that) he is a good person.
   • She thinks (that) he will call her.

# Grammar Check-Up

정답 및 해설 p.18

**01** 다음 중 알맞은 것을 고르시오.

1) I think   if   that   they will go to the bookstore tomorrow.

2) Our team will lose the game   unless   if   we practice harder.

3) If she   will come   comes   tomorrow, we will go to Lotte World together.

**02** 빈칸에 알맞은 접속사를 보기에서 골라 쓰시오.

> 보기        that        unless        if        although

1) _____ it is snowy tomorrow, we will go skiing.

2) I know _____ she cried.

3) You won't catch the bus _____ you hurry up.

3) hurry up 서두르다

**03** 다음 문장을 우리말로 해석하시오.

1) He will be glad if she calls him.

→ _____

2) She wanted to know if he answered the question.

→ _____

3) Unless you study mathematics, you won't pass the math exam.

→ _____

3) mathematics 수학

**04** 우리말과 일치하도록 빈칸에 알맞은 말을 쓰시오.

1) 나는 비록 아팠지만 학교에 갔다.

→ I went to school _____ _____

_____ _____ .

2) 만약 내가 빨리 달리지 않으면 학교에 늦을 것이다.

→ I will be late for school unless _____ _____

_____ .

# 명령문 + and/or, 상관접속사

## A 명령문 + and

~해라, 그러면 …할 것이다

ex • Study hard, and you will get good grades.
    = If you study hard, you will get good grades.

## B 명령문 + or

~해라, 그렇지 않으면 …할 것이다

ex • Study hard, or you will fail the test.
    = If you do not study hard, you will fail the test.
    = Unless you study hard, you will fail the test.

## C 상관접속사

**Tips**
• 상관접속사는 2개 이상의 단어가 모여 접속사 역할을 한다.

1 **both A and B** : A와 B 둘 다 (→ 복수 동사)

ex • Both Jane and I like English.

2 **either A or B** : A이거나 B (→ 동사는 B에 일치)

ex • Either Jane or I am responsible for it.
    • She lost either a pen or a pencil.

3 **neither A nor B** : A도 B도 아닌 (→ 동사는 B에 일치)

ex • Neither Jane nor I am learning French.
    • He is neither a singer nor an actor.

4 **not A but B** : A가 아니고 B (→ 동사는 B에 일치)

ex • Not Jane but I sing well.

5 **not only A but also B = B as well as A** : A뿐만 아니라 B도 (→ 동사는 B에 일치)

ex • Not only Jane but also I study English hard.
    = I as well as Jane study English hard.

**O1** 다음 중 알맞은 것을 고르시오.

1)  Both | Not only   David and I are baseball players.

2)  Either | Neither   David or I have to go to the meeting.

3)  Either | Neither   David nor I am a teacher.

**O2** 두 문장이 같은 뜻이 되도록 빈칸에 알맞은 말을 쓰시오.

1) Have breakfast, or you will be hungry.

= If _____ _____ _____

_____, you will be hungry.

2) She as well as I plays basketball.

= _____ _____ I _____

_____ she _____ basketball.

**O3** 다음 문장을 우리말로 해석하시오.

1) Turn left, and you will see the City Hall.

→ _____

2) Brush your teeth, or you will have tooth decay.

→ _____

3) Neither John nor I saw the movie.

→ _____

2) tooth decay  충치

**O4** 우리말과 일치하도록 빈칸에 알맞은 말을 쓰시오.

1) 너와 나 둘 중 한 명은 옳다.

→ _____ you _____ I _____ right.

2) 그는 선생님이 아니고 학생이다.

→ He is _____ a teacher _____ a student.

3) 앤뿐만 아니라 나도 영어 시험에 통과했다.

→ I _____ _____ _____ Ann

passed the English test.

**[01 - 03] 두 문장의 뜻이 같도록 빈칸에 알맞은 말을 쓰시오.**

01  He was rich, so he could buy a sports car.

= He could buy a sports car _____ he was rich.

02  Ann is wise enough to tell the truth.

= Ann is _____ wise _____ she _____ tell the truth.

03  I don't know if she met him yesterday.

= I don't know _____ she met him yesterday.

04  **밑줄 친 since의 쓰임이 나머지와 다른 것을 고르시오.**

① Since I liked him, I gave him a birthday present.
② Since he was six, he has played football.
③ Since Ann lost the map, she couldn't find the building.
④ Since they are babies, they can't speak.
⑤ Since John ate too much, he got sick.

05  **두 문장의 뜻이 같도록 빈칸에 알맞은 말을 쓰시오.**

If you don't study hard, you will get bad grades.

= _____ you study hard, you will get bad grades.

**[06 - 08] 빈칸에 들어갈 알맞은 것을 고르시오.**

06  She thinks _____ he is good-looking.

① when     ② so      ③ if
④ that     ⑤ while

07  Paul became a professional golfer _____ he was 18.

① when     ② so      ③ if
④ that     ⑤ while

08  _____ Ann had lunch, she was still hungry.

① Since    ② As      ③ If
④ Although  ⑤ So

**[09 - 12] 두 문장의 뜻이 같도록 빈칸에 알맞은 말을 쓰시오.**

09  Hurry up, or you will be late for school.

= Unless _____ _____ _____, you will be late for school.

10  Before she goes to school, she has breakfast.

= _____ she has breakfast, she goes to school.

11  Not only John but also I like tulips.

= I _____ _____ _____ John _____ tulips.

12  He was too tired to play football.

= He was _____ tired _____ he _____ play football.

**13** 밑줄 친 as의 쓰임이 나머지와 <u>다른</u> 것을 고르시오.

① As they felt sleepy, they took a nap.

② As he was in hospital, he couldn't come.

③ As she had a big lunch, she didn't want to have dinner.

④ As I was walking home, I met him.

⑤ As we liked the movie, we saw it twice.

**14** 우리말과 일치하도록 빈칸에 알맞은 말을 쓰시오.

그와 그녀 둘 다 경주에서 이기지 않았다.

→ _____ he _____ she won the race.

**15** 밑줄 친 if의 쓰임이 나머지와 <u>다른</u> 것을 고르시오.

① Have some more if you want.

② Catch me if you can.

③ I don't know if she will come.

④ If my mom comes home earlier, I can go to the movies with you.

⑤ If it is hot tomorrow, we will go to the sea.

**[16-18]** 빈칸에 알맞은 단어를 순서대로 바르게 짝지은 것을 고르시오.

**16**
• I will sleep until my mom _____ me up.
• I want to know if she _____ to the party.

① wakes – will come    ② wakes – come

③ woke – came          ④ will wake – comes

⑤ will wake – will come

**17**
• Both Jane and I _____ singers.
• Either David or I _____ a baseball player.

① are – am    ② are – is    ③ am – am

④ is – is      ⑤ is – am

**18**
• He was hungry, _____ he bought some sandwiches.
• She was wet _____ she didn't have an umbrella.

① because – so         ② because – that

③ so – so              ④ so – because

⑤ because – because

**19** 밑줄 친 부분이 어법상 <u>틀린</u> 것을 고르시오.

① I was tired, so I went to bed earlier.

② I can go out with you when I finish this.

③ Unless you study harder, you will get a good grade.

④ If I finish my homework, I will help you.

⑤ The phone rang while I was taking a bath.

**20** 밑줄 친 when의 쓰임이 나머지와 <u>다른</u> 것을 고르시오.

① When she was a child, she was very shy.

② When you were on Jeju Island, did you climb Mt. Halla?

③ When did you meet him?

④ I will have lunch when I am hungry.

⑤ Call me when you go to the library.

정답 및 해설 p.19

**○1 다음 글의 밑줄 친 부분 중 어법상 틀린 것을 고르시오.**

Beethoven was a German composer. His grandfather and his father ① were also musicians. His father discovered ② that he was talented at music. He gave a concert ③ that he was seven years old. He studied music in Vienna, Austria and settled there. ④ Since some Austrian nobles supported him, he lived a comfortable life. ⑤ Although he loved a woman, he never got married. After he became completely deaf, he kept composing Symphony no. 9 'Choral'.

- composer 작곡가    - settle 정착하다
- support 후원하다    - comfortable 편안한

**○2 다음 괄호 안에서 어법에 맞는 표현으로 가장 적절한 것을 고르시오.**

Jane went to a shop to buy a Christmas present for Tim. She wanted to buy some jeans for Tim but she didn't know A (that / whether) he would like them or not. She wanted some advice from Tim's best friend, David. He told her B (that / whether) Tim needed a pair of glasses, C (because / so) she went to the optician's. There she met Tim, who had already bought a pair of glasses. Tim wanted to go to a discount store to buy a pair of shoes. They went to a discount store and she bought him a pair of shoes.

- optician's 안경점    - discount store 할인점

| A | B | C |
|---|---|---|
| ① whether | – that | – because |
| ② that | – that | – because |
| ③ whether | – whether | – so |
| ④ that | – whether | – so |
| ⑤ whether | – that | – so |

**○1 다음 그림을 보고 빈칸에 알맞은 상관접속사를 쓰시오.**

1)  _____ only Paul _____ _____ Ann had an English book.

2)  _____ Tim nor John arrived in Seoul Station.

**○2 다음 우리말을 읽고 바르게 영작하시오.**

우리는 오늘 날씨가 좋아서 바닷가에 갔다. 우리가 그곳에 도착했을 때가 11시였다. 우리는 점심을 먹을 때까지 수영을 했다. 점심을 먹은 후에, 우리는 모래성을 쌓았다. 그러고 나서 우리는 바닷가를 걸었다. 즐거운 하루였다.

It was sunny today, so we went to the beach.

_____

_____

_____

Then we walked along the beach. It was a

pleasant day.

- build sandcastles 모래성을 쌓다

Chapter

# 12

일치와 화법

## Chapter 미리보기

| 주절(현재) | 종속절(모든 시제) | 주절(과거) | 종속절(과거, 과거완료) |
|---|---|---|---|
| I think | that he was busy.<br>that he is nice.<br>that he will be an actor. | I thought | that he was nice.<br>that he had been busy. |

| 직접화법 | 간접화법 |
|---|---|
| 다른 사람의 말을 그대로 전달 | 남이 말한 내용을 전달하는 사람의 입장으로 바꿔서 전달 |
| He said, "I am hungry."<br>He said to me, "You look pretty." | He said that he was hungry.<br>He told me that I looked pretty. |
| He said to me, "How old are you?"<br>He said to me, "Are you happy?" | He asked me how old I was.<br>He asked me if I was happy. |

One swallow does not make a summer. 제비 한 마리가 여름을 만들지는 않는다.

▶ 너무 조급하게 판단하지 마라.

# Unit 33 시제 일치

시제의 일치란 주절과 종속절로 이루어진 복문에서 주절의 시제와 종속절의 시제를 일치시키는 것을 말한다.

## A 시제 일치의 원칙

주절의 시제가 현재이면 종속절에는 모든 시제가 올 수 있으며, 주절의 시제가 과거이면 종속절에는 과거나 과거완료가 올 수 있다.

| 주절(현재) | 종속절(모든 시제) |
|---|---|
| I know | that he is angry. (→ 현재)<br>that he was busy. (→ 과거)<br>that he will go there. (→ 미래)<br>that he has lost his dog. (→ 현재완료) |

| 주절(과거) | 종속절(과거, 과거 완료) |
|---|---|
| I knew | that he was angry. (→ 과거)<br>that he had been busy. (→ 과거완료)<br>that he would go there. (→ 과거)<br>that he had lost his dog. (→ 과거완료) |

## B 시제 일치의 예외

1 현재의 반복된 습관은 현재시제를 쓴다.

2 일반적 사실, 불변의 진리나 속담, 격언은 현재시제를 쓴다.

3 역사적 사실은 과거시제를 쓴다.

ex • I knew that she goes to work by taxi every day. (습관)
   • My younger brother learned that three times two is six. (일반적 사실)
   • My father said that time is money. (격언)
   • The teacher said that the Korean war ended in 1953. (역사적 사실)

○1 다음 중 알맞은 것을 고르시오.

1) I thought that you   have done | had done   the work.

2) He said that World War II   ended | had ended   in 1945.

3) Karen said that she   doesn't | didn't   like Tim.

4) She told me that her father   will | would   arrive in Seoul.

○2 주절의 시제를 과거시제로 바꿀 때 빈칸에 알맞은 말을 쓰시오.

1) I think that Brian is a good singer.

→ I thought that Brian _____ a good singer.

2) Karen knows that he will attend the meeting.

→ Karen knew that he _____ attend the meeting.

2) attend  참석하다

○3 다음 문장을 우리말로 해석하시오.

1) He thinks that she was very pretty when she was young.

→ _____

2) He thought that she would get well the next day.

→ _____

2) get well
건강이 좋아지다

○4 우리말과 일치하도록 빈칸에 알맞은 말을 쓰시오.

1) 그녀는 태양이 지구보다 크다고 말했다.

→ She said that the Sun _____ _____ than

_____ _____ .

2) 그는 기차를 타겠다고 말했다.

→ He said that _____ would _____

_____ _____ .

# 34 화법 전환

## A 직접화법과 간접화법

직접화법은 다른 사람의 말을 그대로 인용하여 전달하는 것을 말하며, 간접화법은 남이 말한 내용을 전달하는 사람의 입장으로 바꿔서 전달하는 것을 말한다.

ex • He said, "I am sick." (직접화법)
   • He said that he was sick. (간접화법)

## B 평서문의 직접화법을 간접화법으로 바꾸기

① 전달동사를 say/said는 그대로, say/said to는 tell/told로 바꾼다.
② 콤마( , )와 인용부호(" ")를 없애고 that을 쓴다.
③ 인용부호(" ") 안에 있는 인칭대명사는 전달하는 사람에 맞춘다.
④ 시제를 일치시킨다.

ex • He said, "I am happy."
   → He said that he was happy.
   • She said to me, "I want to meet your brother."
   → She told me that she wanted to meet my brother.

## C 의문문의 직접화법을 간접화법으로 바꾸기

① 전달동사는 ask를 쓴다.
② 의문사가 있을 때는 〈의문사 + (주어) + 동사〉가 되며, 의문사가 없을 때는 〈if/whether + 주어 + 동사〉가 된다.
③ 인용부호(" ") 안에 있는 인칭대명사는 전달하는 사람에 맞춘다.
④ 시제를 일치시킨다.

**Tips**
• 의문사가 주어일 경우 〈의문사 + 동사〉가 된다.

ex • He said to her, "Why do you like Brian?"
   → He asked her why she liked Brian.
   • He said to her, "Do you like music?"
   → He asked her if she liked music.
   • He said to me, "Who likes you?"
   → He asked me who liked me.

**01** 다음 중 알맞은 것을 고르시오.

1) Tim  said | asked  that he wanted to take a trip.

2) She  said | told | asked  me that I was handsome.

3) He  said | told | asked  me what time  was it | it was .

1) trip  (짧은) 여행

**02** 다음 문장을 간접화법으로 바꾸어 쓰시오.

1) Mr. Kim said, "I am having a good time."

→ _____

2) He said to me, "I like you."

→ _____

3) She said to him, "Where do you live?"

→ _____

**03** 다음 문장을 우리말로 해석하시오.

1) Tim said, "When does the movie start?"

→ _____

2) Mother asked me if I had taken the medicine.

→ _____

2) medicine  약

**04** 우리말과 일치하도록 빈칸에 알맞은 말을 쓰시오.

1) 그녀는 나에게 "너는 내 지우개를 사용해도 좋아."라고 말했다.

→ She said to me, "_____ may _____

_____ eraser."

2) 그녀는 나에게 그녀의 지우개를 사용해도 좋다고 말했다.

→ She _____ me that _____ might

_____ _____ eraser.

3) 아버지는 그녀에게 몇 살이나고 물으셨다.

→ My father _____ her _____ _____

_____ _____.

# 내신 족집게 문제

**[01-03]** 빈칸에 들어갈 알맞은 것을 고르시오.

**01**
He thought that she _____ in Japan.

① lives　　② has lived　　③ will live
④ lived　　⑤ is living

**02**
She told me that she _____ me.

① calls　　② is calling　　③ will call
④ has called　　⑤ would call

**03**
I learned that the earth _____ around the sun.

① went　　② goes　　③ had gone
④ will go　　⑤ has gone

**[04-05]** 주절의 시제를 과거로 바꾸었을 때 종속절에 들어갈 알맞은 동사를 고르시오.

**04**
I think that she will be a lawyer.
→ I thought that she _____ a lawyer.

① will be　　② is　　③ was
④ would be　　⑤ has been

**05**
He knows that she is honest.
→ He knew that she _____ honest.

① was　　② is　　③ has been
④ would be　　⑤ had been

**06** 빈칸에 공통으로 들어갈 알맞은 동사를 고르시오.

· She _____ many questions of me.
· He _____ me what I wanted to do.

① asked　　② told　　③ said
④ knew　　⑤ thought

**07** 빈칸에 들어갈 알맞은 것을 고르시오.

My teacher asked me _____ I could play the flute.

① that　　② and　　③ but
④ so　　⑤ if

**08** 빈칸에 알맞은 단어를 순서대로 바르게 짝지은 것을 고르시오.

· My mom _____ that she was cooking dinner.
· My mom _____ me that I had to study hard.

① asked - told　　② said – told
③ told – said　　④ said – asked
⑤ told – asked

**09** 다음 중 간접화법으로 잘못 바꾼 문장을 고르시오.

① He said to me, "You can have the book."
　→ He told me that I could have the book.
② She said to him, "I want to meet you."
　→ She told him that she wanted to meet him.
③ They said to her, "What are you doing?"
　→ They asked her what she was doing.
④ My dad said to her, "Where will you be?"
　→ My dad asked her where would she be.
⑤ She said to me, "Are you happy?"
　→ She asked me if I was happy.

**10** 밑줄 친 부분이 어법상 틀린 것을 고르시오.

① He said that Columbus had discovered America in 1492.
② She said that honesty is the best policy.
③ Tim told me that he washes his car every Sunday.
④ She said that he would finish his work.
⑤ The teacher said that China is in Asia.

**[11-13]** 다음 문장을 간접화법으로 바꿀 때 빈칸에 알맞은 말을 쓰시오.

**11** He said to me, "You look pretty."

→ He _____ me that _____ _____ pretty.

**12** I said to the girl, "Where are you from?"

→ I _____ the girl _____ _____ _____ from.

**13** She said to me, "May I use your cell phone?"

→ She _____ me _____ _____ might _____ my cell phone.

**14** 다음 문장을 간접화법 문장으로 바르게 바꾼 것을 고르시오.

He said to her, "Who likes you?"

① He told her who liked her.
② He asked her who she liked.
③ He told her who she liked.
④ He asked her who liked her.
⑤ He said her who liked her.

**[15-17]** 빈칸에 들어갈 알맞은 것을 고르시오.

**15** She says, "I will keep my promise."

→ She says that _____.

① she would keep my promise
② she will keep her promise
③ I will keep my promise
④ she would keep her promise
⑤ she kept her promise

**16** She said to the man, "Where do you work?"

→ She asked the man _____.

① that where he worked
② where you worked
③ where did he work
④ where he worked
⑤ where he did worked

**17** I asked him if he was married

→ I said to him "_____ married?"

① Is he        ② Was he        ③ Are you
④ Were you        ⑤ You are

**18** 우리말을 바르게 영작한 것을 고르시오.

나의 선생님께서는 지구는 둥글다고 말씀하셨다.

① My teacher said that the earth is round.
② My teacher said that the earth was round.
③ My teacher told that the earth is round.
④ My teacher told that the earth was round.
⑤ My teacher said that the earth will be round.

**[19-20]** 우리말과 일치하도록 빈칸에 알맞은 말을 쓰시오.

**19** 그녀는 나에게 키가 몇인지 물어보았다.

→ She asked me _____ _____ _____ _____.

**20** 그녀는 그녀의 어머니가 아프다고 말했다.

→ She said _____ _____ _____ _____ _____.

# 수능 감각 기르기

# 서술형 즐기기

O1 다음 글의 밑줄 친 부분 중 어법상 <u>틀린</u> 것을 고르시오.

> Yesterday I went to Hyundae department store with my friend to buy shoes. When we got there, we didn't know ① where we should go. My friend asked a clerk ② where could she buy shoes. She ③ told us that the shoe stores were on the fourth floor. There were ④ a lot of shoe stores there. I found ⑤ some pairs of shoes that I liked, but they were too expensive to buy. We went to the nearby market.

O1 다음 문장을 보기처럼 간접화법 문장으로 쓰시오.

> 보기 "I am fine."
> → She said that she was fine.

1) "I am going to the library."

→ She said _____.

2) "I have a test."

→ She said _____.

3) "I will call you."

→ She told me _____.

O2 다음 빈칸에 들어갈 말로 가장 적절한 것을 고르시오.

> It was my first day as an English teacher. When I entered the classroom, the students were having a chat. I stood in front of the teacher's desk and waited for them to be quiet. When the students stopped talking, I introduced myself to them. Some of the students raised their hands to ask questions. A student asked A_____. Another student asked if I was single. The third student B_____ me if I had a boyfriend. The students didn't stop C_____ questions. I spent most of the first class answering their questions.

■ introduce 소개하다　■ single 독신인

| | A | B | C |
|---|---|---|---|
| ① | how old I was | asked | asking |
| ② | how old I was | told | asking |
| ③ | how old I was | asked | to ask |
| ④ | how old was I | told | asking |
| ⑤ | how old was I | asked | asking |

O2 다음 우리말을 읽고 바르게 영작하시오.

나는 울고 있는 아이를 만났다. 나는 왜 울고 있는지 물어보았다. 나는 그에게 어디에 사는지도 물어보았다. 놀랍게도 그는 나의 옆집에 산다고 말했다.

_____

_____

_____

_____

_____

■ surprisingly 놀랍게도

Chapter 13

가정법

## Chapter 미리보기

|  | 실현 가능성 | 문장 형식 |
|---|---|---|
| **가정법 현재** | ○ | If + 주어 + 현재, 주어 + will/can + 동사원형 |
| **가정법 과거** | ✕ | If + 주어 + 과거, 주어 + would/could + 동사원형 |
| **가정법 과거완료** | ✕ | If + 주어 + 과거완료, 주어 + would/could + have p.p |

▶ 한 우물만 파라.

# 35 가정법 현재와 과거

## A 가정법 현재

현재나 미래에 대한 불확실한 상황을 가정하는 구문이다.

> If + 주어 + 동사의 현재형/동사원형, 주어 + will/can + 동사원형
> → 만약 ~면, …할 것이다

**ex** • If he calls me, I will be happy. (그가 전화한다면, 나는 행복할 것이다.)
 • If she is honest, I will employ her.

**Tips**
• 직설법은 사실인 경우에 사용하고 가정법은 상상할 경우나 사실이 아닌 경우에 사용한다.
• 가정법 과거는 직설법 현재로 바꿀 수 있다.

## B 가정법 과거

현재 사실과 다른 일이나 실현 가능성이 희박한 일을 나타낸다.

> If + 주어 + 동사의 과거형/were, 주어 + would/could + 동사원형
> → 만약 ~면, …할 텐데

**ex** • If I were an American, I could speak English fluently.
 → As I am not an American, I cannot speak English fluently.

 • If I had time, I would watch TV.
 → As I don't have time, I don't watch TV.

 • If Ann were here, I could play with her.
 → As Ann is not here, I can't play with her.

 • If I had the book, I could lend it to you.
 → As I don't have the book, I can't lend it to you.

## C 가정법 현재와 가정법 과거의 비교

| 가정법 현재<br>(실현 가능성 有) | If it is sunny tomorrow, we will go on a picnic.<br>만약 내일 날씨가 화창하면, 우리는 소풍을 갈 것이다. |
|---|---|
| 가정법 과거<br>(실현 가능성 無) | If it were sunny, we would go on a picnic.<br>지금 날씨가 화창하면, 우리는 소풍을 갈 텐데. |

○1 주어진 단어를 알맞은 형태로 바꾸어 빈칸에 쓰시오.

1) If she _____ early, she will bake a cake. (come)

2) If I _____ money, I would buy the book. (have)

3) If they invited her, she _____ _____
to the party. (will, come)

3) invite  초대하다

○2 두 문장의 뜻이 같도록 빈칸에 알맞은 말을 쓰시오.

1) As we don't have time, we can't play football.

= If we _____ time, we _____ _____
football.

2) As I am not a singer, I can't sing well.

= If I _____ a singer, I _____ _____
well.

○3 다음 문장을 우리말로 해석하시오.

1) If it is hot tomorrow, we will go to the beach.

→ _____

2) If it were hot, we would go to the beach.

→ _____

○4 우리말과 일치하도록 주어진 말을 바르게 배열하시오.

1) 내가 그를 안다면, 그와 이야기를 할 텐데.

(I, if, talk to, him, would, knew, I, him)

→ _____

2) 그녀가 그를 좋아한다면, 그는 행복할 텐데.

(he, him, liked, happy, if, be, she, would)

→ _____

# 36 가정법 과거완료

## A 가정법 과거완료

과거 사실과 다른 일이나 과거에 실현하지 못한 일을 가정해서 말할 때 사용한다.

> If + 주어 + had p.p, 주어 + would/could have p.p
> → 만약 ~했다면, …했을 텐데

**ex** • If I had finished my homework, I would have gone to the movies.
  (내가 숙제를 마쳤다면, 영화를 보러 갈 수 있었을 텐데.)
  (→ 과거의 그 당시에 숙제를 다 못해서 영화를 보러 가지 못했다는 뜻)

• If she had studied harder, she would have passed the test.
  (그녀가 더 열심히 공부했더라면, 그 시험에 통과했을 텐데.)
  (→ 과거에 공부를 열심히 안 해서 시험에 통과하지 못했다는 뜻)

• If she had known the answer, she could have won the first prize.
  (그녀가 정답을 알았더라면, 일등상을 받았을 텐데.)
  = As she didn't know the answer, she couldn't win the first prize.
    (그녀는 정답을 몰라서 일등상을 받을 수 없었다.)

• If he had met her, he would have made friends with her.
  (그가 그녀를 만났다면, 그녀와 친구가 될 수 있었을 텐데.)
  = As he didn't meet her, he didn't make friends with her.
    (그는 그녀를 만나지 않아서 그녀와 친구가 되지 않았다.)

## B 가정법 현재, 가정법 과거, 가정법 과거완료

|  | 실현 가능성 | 문장 형식 |
|---|---|---|
| **가정법 현재** | ○ | If + 주어 + 현재, 주어 + will/can + 동사원형<br>(만약 ~면, …할 것이다) |
| **가정법 과거** | × | If + 주어 + 과거, 주어 + would/could + 동사원형<br>(만약 ~면, …할 텐데) |
| **가정법 과거완료** | × | If + 주어 + 과거완료, 주어 + would/could + have p.p<br>(만약 ~했다면, …했을 텐데) |

**01** 다음 중 알맞은 것을 고르시오.

1) If I didn't have any homework, I   watched / would watch   TV.

2) If I   had / had had   a lot of money, I could have traveled around the world.

**02** 두 문장의 뜻이 같도록 빈칸에 알맞은 말을 쓰시오.

1) As I didn't have money, I couldn't buy some lilies.

   = If I _____ _____ money, I _____

   _____ _____ some lilies.

2) As she is not here, I can't play with her.

   = If she _____ here, I _____ _____

   with her.

1) lily 백합

**03** 다음 문장을 우리말로 해석하시오.

1) If he had come to the party, he would have met her.

   → _____

2) If I were a teacher, I would give students less homework.

   → _____

**04** 우리말과 일치하도록 주어진 말을 바르게 배열하시오.

1) 우리가 저녁을 먹었더라면, 우리는 배가 고프지 않았을 텐데.

   (we, dinner, if, had, have, we, been hungry, wouldn't, had)

   → _____

2) 그들이 우리를 돕는다면, 우리는 그 일을 일찍 끝낼 수 있을 텐데.

   (they, could, the work, finish, we, helped, if, us, early)

   → _____

# 내신 족집게 문제

**[01-02]** 주어진 단어를 알맞은 형태로 바꾸어 빈칸에 쓰시오.

01  If she _____ her homework, she would go to the movies. (finish)

02  If he _____ her, he would have talked to her. (know)

**[03-05]** 밑줄 친 부분이 어법상 **틀린** 것을 고르시오.

03  If she knows the answer, she would tell it to him.
    ①  ②   ③     ④  ⑤

04  If he has a car, he could have gone to the market.
    ①   ②  ③       ④  ⑤

05  If it were sunny tomorrow, I will play football
    ①  ②   ③       ④

with my friends.
     ⑤

**[06-08]** 두 문장의 뜻이 같도록 빈칸에 알맞은 말을 쓰시오.

06  As it is not snowing, we can't make a snowman.

= If it _____ snowing, we could make a snowman.

07  As he fell down, he couldn't win a gold medal.

= If he _____ _____ down, he could have won a gold medal.

08  Study hard, and you will get good grades.

= _____ you study hard, you _____ get good grades.

**[09-11]** 빈칸에 알맞은 단어를 순서대로 바르게 짝지은 것을 고르시오.

09  만약 내일 비가 온다면, 그들은 집에서 TV를 볼 것이다.
→ If it _____ rainy tomorrow, they _____ TV at home.

① is – watch　　　　② is – will watch
③ were – watch　　　④ were – will watch
⑤ were – watched

10  만약 내게 돈이 없었다면, 집에 걸어가야 했을 텐데.
→ If I _____ any money, I _____ home.

① didn't have – will walk
② didn't have – walked
③ hadn't had – walked
④ hadn't had – would have walked
⑤ hadn't had – will walk

11  만약 내게 친구가 없다면, 외로울 텐데,
→ If I _____ any friends, I _____ lonely.

① didn't have – would be
② didn't have – will be
③ hadn't had – was
④ hadn't had – would have been
⑤ hadn't had – will be

12  다음 중 올바른 문장을 고르시오.

① If she didn't sing well, she could be a singer.
② If he had had some money, he couldn't have bought the pen.
③ If it were snowy, we will go skiing.
④ If we were Americans, we wouldn't speak English fluently.
⑤ If you eat too much, you will have a stomachache.

13 두 문장의 뜻이 같지 <u>않은</u> 것을 고르시오.

① If I were you, I would call him.
= As I am not you, I won't call him.

② If she had known his address, she would have written him a letter.
= As she didn't know his address, she didn't write him a letter.

③ If it were windy, we would go wind-surfing.
= As it isn't windy, we will go wind-surfing.

④ If I were a cook, I could make a delicious meal.
= As I am not a cook, I can't make a delicious meal.

⑤ If he had studied math, he could have answered the question.
= As he didn't study math, he couldn't answer the question.

**[14 - 16] 우리말과 일치하도록 빈칸에 알맞은 말을 쓰시오.**

14 만약 내가 키가 크다면, 농구를 잘 할 수 있을 텐데.

→ If I _____ tall, I _____
_____ basketball well.

15 만약 우리가 집에 있었더라면, 그를 만날 수 있었을 텐데.

→ If we _____ _____ at home, we
_____ _____ _____ him.

16 만약 그들이 일찍 온다면, 나는 기쁠 것이다.

→ If they _____ earlier, I _____
_____ glad.

17 다음 중 어법상 <u>틀린</u> 문장을 고르시오.

① If I were a magician, I could turn it into a rabbit.

② If you tell a lie, your friend will be disappointed.

③ If we didn't meet her, we would buy her lunch.

④ If you get up late, you can't have breakfast.

⑤ If I had seen him, I would have waved to him.

**[18 - 19] 다음 중 보기와 의미가 같은 문장을 고르시오.**

18 보기 If she weren't ill, she would go to the party.

① As she was ill, she will go to the party.

② As she wasn't ill, she won't go to the party.

③ As she isn't ill, she will go to the party.

④ As she is ill, she will go to the party.

⑤ As she is ill, she won't go to the party.

19 보기 As he lost his car key, he couldn't use his car.

① If he didn't lose his car key, he could use his car.

② If he didn't lose his car key, he can use his car.

③ If he lost his car key, he can't use his car.

④ If he hadn't lost his car key, he could have used his car.

⑤ If he hadn't lost his car key, he couldn't have used his car.

20 두 문장의 뜻이 같도록 빈칸에 알맞은 말을 쓰시오.

If you don't walk fast, you won't get there on time.

= _____ you walk fast, you won't get there on time.

정답 및 해설 p.22

**O1** 다음 글의 밑줄 친 부분 중 어법상 틀린 것을 고르시오.

I am a fan of Jisung Park. He played for Manchester United of the English Premier league. If I ① had been to England, I would have watched him play. ② Although he is flat footed, he runs without ③ stopping. He said he didn't know he was flat footed. During training, he felt pain in his feet but he never stopped ④ training. He even trained more to overcome his disadvantages. If he ⑤ gave up training, he wouldn't have become a world famous football payer.

■ overcome 극복하다　　■ disadvantage 단점, 약점

**O1** 가정법 문장이 되도록 빈칸에 알맞은 말을 쓰시오.

David : If I learn a trick today, I _____ tell you. Wow! Look at the picture of the flying carpet. _____ _____ _____ a magician, I could use a flying carpet. It would be wonderful!

Jane　: Look at the magic wand! _____ _____ _____ that magic wand, I could turn you into a dove. It would be fun!

■ magician 마술사　　■ magic wand 마법의 지팡이

**O2** 다음 괄호 안에서 어법에 맞는 표현으로 가장 적절한 것을 고르시오.

I failed an English test last month. If I Ⓐ(studied / had studied) harder, I would have passed the test. Now I study English three hours a day. It is hard work! If I Ⓑ(am / were) an American, I wouldn't study English so hard. My English teacher said my English was improving. If I Ⓒ(had / have) another chance to take an English test, I will get a better result.

|  | Ⓐ |  | Ⓑ |  | Ⓒ |
|---|---|---|---|---|---|
| ① studied | – | were | – | had |
| ② had studied | – | am | – | have |
| ③ studied | – | am | – | had |
| ④ had studied | – | were | – | have |
| ⑤ studied | – | were | – | have |

**O2** 다음 우리말을 읽고 바르게 영작하시오.

일주일 동안 계속 비가 오고 있다. 만약 어제 비가 오지 않았다면, 우리는 에버랜드에 갔을 텐데. 만약 지금 비가 오지 않는다면, 우리는 축구를 할 텐데. 만약 내일 비가 온다면, 우리는 집에 머무를 것이다.

It has been raining for a week.

_____

_____

_____

# 불규칙
# 동사 변화표

# 불규칙 동사 변화표

| 현재 | 과거 | 과거분사 | 현재 | 과거 | 과거분사 |
|---|---|---|---|---|---|
| **be** 이다, 있다 | was, were | been | **fly** 날다 | flew | flown |
| **become** 되다 | became | become | **forget** 잊다 | forgot | forgotten |
| **begin** 시작하다 | began | begun | **forgive** 용서하다 | forgave | forgiven |
| **bite** 물다 | bit | bitten | **get** 얻다 | got | got(gotten) |
| **break** 깨다 | broke | broken | **give** 주다 | gave | given |
| **bring** 가지고 오다 | brought | brought | **go** 가다 | went | gone |
| **build** (건물) 짓다 | built | built | **grow** 자라다 | grew | grown |
| **buy** 사다 | bought | bought | **have** 가지고 있다, 먹다 | had | had |
| **catch** 잡다 | caught | caught | **hear** 듣다 | heard | heard |
| **choose** 선택하다 | chose | chosen | **keep** 유지하다 | kept | kept |
| **come** 오다 | came | come | **know** 알다 | knew | known |
| **cut** 자르다 | cut | cut | **leave** 떠나다 | left | left |
| **do** 하다 | did | done | **lend** 빌려주다 | lent | lent |
| **drink** 마시다 | drank | drunk | **lose** 잃어버리다 | lost | lost |
| **drive** 운전하다 | drove | driven | **make** 만들다 | made | made |
| **eat** 먹다 | ate | eaten | **meet** 만나다 | met | met |
| **fall** 떨어지다 | fell | fallen | **pay** 지불하다 | paid | paid |
| **feed** 먹이를 주다 | fed | fed | **put** 놓다 | put | put |
| **feel** 느끼다 | felt | felt | **read** 읽다 | read | read |
| **find** 찾다 | found | found | **ring** (종 등이) 울리다 | rang | rung |

| 현재 | 과거 | 과거분사 |
|---|---|---|
| run 달리다 | ran | run |
| say 말하다 | said | said |
| see 보다 | saw | seen |
| sell 팔다 | sold | sold |
| send 보내다 | sent | sent |
| shake 흔들다 | shook | shaken |
| sing 노래하다 | sang | sung |
| sit 앉다 | sat | sat |
| sleep 잠자다 | slept | slept |
| spend 소비하다 | spent | spent |
| stand 서 있다 | stood | stood |
| speak 말하다 | spoke | spoken |
| steal 훔치다 | stole | stolen |
| swim 수영하다 | swam | swum |
| take 가지고 가다 | took | taken |
| teach 가르치다 | taught | taught |
| think 생각하다 | thought | thought |
| wear 입다 | wore | worn |
| win 이기다 | won | won |
| write 쓰다 | wrote | written |

불규칙이니까
무조건
외워야 해!

## 다음 동사의 과거형과 과거분사형을 써보세요.

| 현재 | 과거 | 과거분사 |
|------|------|----------|
| be 이다, 있다 | | |
| become 되다 | | |
| begin 시작하다 | | |
| bite 물다 | | |
| break 깨다 | | |
| bring 가지고 오다 | | |
| build (건물) 짓다 | | |
| buy 사다 | | |
| catch 잡다 | | |
| choose 선택하다 | | |
| come 오다 | | |
| cut 자르다 | | |
| do 하다 | | |
| drink 마시다 | | |
| drive 운전하다 | | |
| eat 먹다 | | |
| fall 떨어지다 | | |
| feed 먹이를 주다 | | |
| feel 느끼다 | | |
| find 찾다 | | |

| 현재 | 과거 | 과거분사 |
|------|------|----------|
| fly 날다 | | |
| forget 잊다 | | |
| forgive 용서하다 | | |
| get 얻다 | | |
| give 주다 | | |
| go 가다 | | |
| grow 자라다 | | |
| have 가지고 있다, 먹다 | | |
| hear 듣다 | | |
| keep 유지하다 | | |
| know 알다 | | |
| leave 떠나다 | | |
| lend 빌려주다 | | |
| lose 잃어버리다 | | |
| make 만들다 | | |
| meet 만나다 | | |
| pay 지불하다 | | |
| put 놓다 | | |
| read 읽다 | | |
| ring (종 등이) 울리다 | | |

| 현재 | 과거 | 과거분사 |
| --- | --- | --- |
| run 달리다 | | |
| say 말하다 | | |
| see 보다 | | |
| sell 팔다 | | |
| send 보내다 | | |
| shake 흔들다 | | |
| sing 노래하다 | | |
| sit 앉다 | | |
| sleep 잠자다 | | |
| spend 소비하다 | | |
| stand 서 있다 | | |
| speak 말하다 | | |
| steal 훔치다 | | |
| swim 수영하다 | | |
| take 가지고 가다 | | |
| teach 가르치다 | | |
| think 생각하다 | | |
| wear 입다 | | |
| win 이기다 | | |
| write 쓰다 | | |

꽉! 잡은 중학 영문법

**2** Book

# GRAMMAR
# CATCH

**저자** 김명이 · 이재림

**초판 1쇄 발행** 2007년 7월 12일
**개정판 1쇄 발행** 2015년 6월 20일
**개정판 6쇄 발행** 2022년 8월 30일

**편집장** 조미자
**책임편집** 류은정 · 권민정 · 김미경 · 정진희 · 최수경
**표지디자인** 김교빈
**디자인** 김교빈 · 임미영
**관리** 이성희 · 신세영 · 신시아
**인쇄** 삼화 인쇄

**펴낸이** 정규도
**펴낸곳** Happy House
**주소** 경기도 파주시 문발로 211 다락원 빌딩
**전화** 02-736-2031 (내선 250)
**팩스** 02-732-2037
**출판등록** 1977년 9월 16일 제406-2008-000007호

ISBN 978-89-6653-188-2 53740

**값 12,000원**

[Grammar Catch] 시리즈는 [오! 마이 그래머] 시리즈의 개정 증보판입니다.

**정답 및 해설 무료 다운로드** www.ihappyhouse.co.kr
*Happy House는 다락원의 임프린트입니다.

꾹! 잡은 중학 영문법

# GRAMMAR CATCH

Book 2

★ Workbook ★

Happy House

꽉! 잡은 중학 영문법

**2** Book

# GRAMMAR
# CATCH
## ★ Workbook ★

## Contents

**O1** 다음 중 알맞은 것을 고르시오.

1) Water   boils ǀ boiled ǀ will boil   at 100℃.

2) The Vietnam War   ends ǀ ended ǀ will end   in 1975.

3) He   goes ǀ went ǀ will go   abroad to study next year.

4) Brian's aunt   makes ǀ made ǀ will make   the special meal last Thanksgiving Day.

5) My father   attends ǀ attended ǀ will attend   a seminar on environment next week.

6) If it   will snow ǀ snows ǀ snowed   tomorrow, we will make a snowman.

**O2** 주어진 말을 알맞은 형태로 바꾸어 빈칸에 쓰시오.

1) She _____ a member of an orchestra when she was young.   (be)

2) I _____ an apple tree tomorrow.   (plant)

3) He _____ his teeth three times a day.   (brush)

4) Bora _____ a cake and some wine yesterday.   (buy)

5) A diamond _____ a hard, bright, and precious stone.   (be)

6) Shakespeare _____ *Romeo and Juliet*.   (write)

7) She _____ many books in her room now.   (have)

8) When he _____ here, we will give him these flowers.   (arrive)

**O3** 우리말과 일치하도록 빈칸에 알맞은 말을 쓰시오.

1) 보미는 지난 주말에 탁구를 쳤다.

→ Bomi _____ table tennis last weekend.

2) 그녀는 매일 아침 샤워를 한다.

→ She _____ a shower every morning.

3) 나는 친구에게 크리스마스 선물을 보낼 것이다.

→ I _____ _____ a Christmas gift to my friend.

4) 그는 그녀가 돌아올 때까지 여기서 기다릴 것이다.

→ He _____ _____ here until she _____ back.

5) 내 친구들 중 한 명이 3년 전에 시카고로 이사 갔다.

→ One of my friends _____ to Chicago three years ago.

6) 그 고구마는 매우 좋은 냄새가 난다.

→ The sweet potato _____ very good.

○4 주어진 말을 이용하여 질문에 대한 대답을 쓰시오.

1) Ⓐ What did you do last weekend?

Ⓑ _____ (have an online chat)

2) Ⓐ What does your mother do every night?

Ⓑ _____ (watch TV dramas)

3) Ⓐ What is she going to do tomorrow morning?

Ⓑ _____ (ride a bike along the river)

4) Ⓐ What will you do this weekend?

Ⓑ _____ (meet my old friends)

○5 밑줄 친 부분을 바르게 고쳐 쓰시오.

1) I meet her on my way home two days ago.　　　(→ _____ )

2) Paris was the capital of France.　　　(→ _____ )

3) World War II breaks out in 1939.　　　(→ _____ )

4) He arrived in Seoul at 8 tomorrow.　　　(→ _____ )

5) The sun rose in the east.　　　(→ _____ )

6) Her father had two houses in Jejudo now.　　　(→ _____ )

7) They don't take a lot of pictures of their baby last week.　　　(→ _____ )

8) If it was sunny tomorrow, we will take a walk outside.　　　(→ _____ )

○6 주어진 말을 이용하여 다음 우리말을 영작하시오.

1) 브라운 씨(Mrs. Brown)는 일주일에 두 번 수영하러 간다. (go swimming)

→ _____

2) 그는 5년 전에 이 집을 샀다. (ago)

→ _____

3) 그녀는 매일마다 아침으로 밥을 먹는다. (for breakfast, rice)

→ _____

4) 나는 이번 주 토요일에 신발 한 켤레를 살 것이다. (a pair of shoes, this Saturday)

→ _____

5) 만약에 내일 그녀가 오면 우리는 외식할 것이다. (if, eat out)

→ _____

6) 우리는 지난 주말에 그녀의 생일 파티를 열었다. (have her birthday party)

→ _____

**01** 다음 중 알맞은 것을 고르시오.

1) My sister   is playing | was playing | playing   the cello now.

2) He   is taking | was taking | taking   a shower when I visited him.

3) Mr. Smith   is having | has | have   two cats in his house.

4) We   are having | has | have   bread for lunch now.

5) The spaghetti   is tasting | tastes | tasting   very delicious.

6) My brother   is tasting | tastes | tasting   the spaghetti now.

7) My father   is driving | was driving | driving   a car at that time.

8) They   are playing | play | playing   soccer after school every day.

9) They   are playing | play | playing   baseball now.

**02** 주어진 말을 이용하여 질문에 대한 대답을 쓰시오.

1) Ⓐ What are you doing now?

Ⓑ _____ (cook dinner)

2) Ⓐ What is your mother doing?

Ⓑ _____ (swim in the pool)

3) Ⓐ What were you doing then?

Ⓑ _____ (write an email)

4) Ⓐ What was your brother doing then?

Ⓑ _____ (read comic books)

**03** 우리말과 일치하도록 빈칸에 알맞은 말을 쓰시오.

1) 우리는 지금 중국어를 배우고 있다.

→ We _____ _____ Chinese now.

2) 네가 전화했을 때 나는 게임을 하고 있었어.

→ When you called me up, I _____ _____ a game.

3) 그의 어머니는 카페에서 커피를 마시고 있다.

→ His mother _____ _____ coffee at the cafe.

4) 그 아이는 그때 그의 어머니를 기다리고 있었다.

→ The kid _____ _____ for his mother then.

**04** 다음 문장의 <u>틀린</u> 부분에 밑줄을 긋고 바르게 고쳐 쓰시오.

1) The fried chicken is smelling very good. (→ _____ )

2) Many foreigners taking pictures now. (→ _____ )

3) Is your mother make cookies in the kitchen now? (→ _____ )

4) This house is belonging to my uncle. (→ _____ )

5) She is watching news on TV at 9 yesterday. (→ _____ )

**05** 우리말과 일치하도록 주어진 말을 바르게 배열하시오.

1) 우리는 지금 영어 시험을 보고 있다.

(are, an English test, taking, we, at the moment)

→ _____

2) 그녀가 방으로 들어왔을 때 나는 TV를 보고 있었다.

(she, when, watching, I, the room, was, entered, TV)

→ _____

3) 그의 친구는 잃어버린 강아지를 거리에서 찾고 있다.

(his, looking, friend, is, for, a, on, lost puppy, the street)

→ _____

4) 나는 어젯밤 11시에 내 친구와 전화 통화를 하고 있었다.

(was, I, talking, my friend, on, with, the phone, 11, last night, at)

→ _____

5) 너는 지금 집에서 너의 여동생을 돌보고 있니?

(sister, you, taking, are, home, care, now, of, your, at, ?)

→ _____

**06** 주어진 말을 이용하여 다음 우리말을 영작하시오.

1) 나의 여동생은 잠자리 한 마리를 따라가고 있다. (dragonfly, follow)

→ _____

2) 그들은 그때 운동장에서 야구를 하고 있었다. (on the playground)

→ _____

3) 크리스(Chris)는 지금 우리를 위해서 스파게티를 요리하는 중이다. (spaghetti)

→ _____

4) 초인종이 울렸을 때 나는 음악을 듣고 있었다. (doorbell, rang)

→ _____

**O1** 주어진 말을 이용하여 현재완료 문장을 완성하시오.

1) _____ to Jejudo? (you, ever, be)

2) They _____ math for two hours. (study)

3) Bora and I _____ cleaning the house. (just, finish)

4) He _____ for France. (already, leave)

5) We _____ our homework yet. (not, do)

6) I _____ Jennifer since last Friday. (not, see)

7) My father _____ his favorite wallet. (lose)


**O2** 다음 문장을 우리말로 해석하고 현재완료의 용법(경험, 계속, 완료, 결과)을 쓰시오.

1) He has never been to Austria before.

→ _____ ( _____ )

2) Her bus has just arrived at the bus stop.

→ _____ ( _____ )

3) It has been rainy for a week.

→ _____ ( _____ )

4) We have known the writer since we were young.

→ _____ ( _____ )

5) Her boyfriend has gone to Germany.

→ _____ ( _____ )

6) Have they finished cooking dinner yet?

→ _____ ( _____ )


**O3** 다음 중 알맞은 것을 고르시오.

1) She   was | has been   busy yesterday.

2) She   was | has been   busy since yesterday.

3) My brother   has not believed | didn't believe   in Santa Claus since last year.

4) He   finished | has finished   the project last year.

5) I have   been | gone   to London once.

6) They   stayed | have stayed   at the hotel a week ago.

7) They   stayed | have stayed   at this hotel for a week.

8) The weather has been hot   for | since   last Sunday.

○4 밑줄 친 부분을 바르게 고쳐 쓰시오.

1) We live in this apartment for ten years. (→ _____ )

2) Have you ever visit Harvard University? (→ _____ )

3) I have gone to Tokyo. (→ _____ )

4) A: Has your sister taught English before?  B: Yes, she does. (→ _____ )

5) A: What have you done for an hour?  B: I played the cello. (→ _____ )

6) She has learned Spanish two years ago. (→ _____ )

7) When have you read *Harry Potter*? (→ _____ )

8) They don't have sent an invitation card to Sam yet. (→ _____ )

○5 다음 두 문장을 한 문장으로 나타낼 때 빈칸에 들어갈 알맞은 말을 쓰시오.

1) Sora lost her cell phone. She doesn't have it now.

→ Sora _____ _____ her cell phone.

2) He went to China. He is not back yet.

→ He _____ _____ to China.

3) They moved to Canada five years ago. They still live there.

→ They _____ _____ in Canada for five years.

4) She was sick yesterday. She is still sick.

→ She _____ _____ sick _____ yesterday.

○6 주어진 말을 이용하여 다음 우리말을 영작하시오.

1) 너는 이탈리아에 가 본 적이 있니? (Italy)

→ _____

2) 너는 언제 진짜 코알라를 봤니? (real koala, see)

→ _____

3) 그녀는 이미 저녁을 먹었다. (already)

→ _____

4) 나의 남동생은 10년 동안 그 여배우를 좋아해 왔다. (actress)

→ _____

5) 당신은 한국에 계신 지 얼마나 되었습니까? (how long, be)

→ _____

6) 그 기차는 5분 전에 떠났다. (minutes)

→ _____

**01** 밑줄 친 부분을 바르게 고쳐 쓰시오.

1) Would you like have some more pizza?　　　　(→ _____ )

2) She will can sing at that concert.　　　　　　(→ _____ )

3) He can be an American. He doesn't speak English.　(→ _____ )

4) Dad stopped smoking, so he will smoke again.　(→ _____ )


**02** 다음 문장을 지시대로 바꾸어 쓰시오.

1) Suzie will learn Chinese next month.

　 부정문 ▶ _____

2) They can make an internet cafe for their club.

　 과거시제 ▶ _____

3) We can answer these difficult math questions.

　 미래시제 ▶ _____


**03** 보기와 주어진 말을 이용하여 문장을 완성하시오.

| 보기 | can | will | won't |

1) Ann lived in France for three years. So she _____ French well.　(speak)

2) I don't like the bag. So I _____ it.　(buy)

3) Susan has a bad cold. So she _____ to bed early.　(go)


**04** 두 문장의 뜻이 같도록 빈칸에 알맞은 말을 쓰시오.

1) She can't help me with my homework.

　 = She _____ _____ _____ help me with my homework.

2) Are they able to climb Mt. Everest?

　 = _____ they climb Mt. Everest?

3) We are going to go camping with them.

　 = We _____ go camping with them.

4) My sister would like to buy a pair of shoes.

　 = My sister _____ _____ buy a pair of shoes.

**05 다음 문장을 우리말로 해석하시오.**

1) She is able to speak English fluently.

→ _____

2) You can use my headphones.

→ _____

3) The news may be wrong.

→ _____

4) Susan can't be his sister.

→ _____

5) May I go with you?

→ _____


**06 우리말과 일치하도록 주어진 말을 바르게 배열하시오.**

1) 우리는 다음주에 런던에 갈 예정이다. (go, week, going, London, are, to, next, we, to)

→ _____

2) 그는 자동차를 운전할 수 없다. (is, drive, not, to, car, he, able, a)

→ _____

3) 너는 오늘 오후에 내 컴퓨터를 사용해도 된다. (my, use, afternoon, you, computer, can, this)

→ _____

4) 케이크 좀 더 드시겠어요? (cake, you, some, have, like, would, more, to)

→ _____


**07 주어진 말을 이용하여 다음 우리말을 영작하시오.**

1) 방을 나가도 되겠습니까? (leave)

→ _____

2) 그는 음악 선생님일 리 없다. (be)

→ _____

3) 해리(Harry)는 직업을 찾을 수 있을 것이다. (find a job)

→ _____

4) 나는 일기를 쓰지 않을 것이다. (keep a diary)

→ _____

# Unit 05 ▶ must, have to, should, had better

**01** 다음 문장의 틀린 부분에 밑줄을 긋고 바르게 고쳐 쓰시오.

1) We had not better tell a lie. (→ _____ )

2) She doesn't has to worry about it. (→ _____ )

3) He will must go to the army next month. (→ _____ )

4) She has to eating more vegetables. (→ _____ )

**02** 다음 문장을 지시대로 바꾸어 쓰시오.

1) He must hand in an English essay today.

　의문문 ▶ _____

2) She must solve the problem alone.

　과거시제 ▶ _____

3) They must go to the Seoul Library.

　미래시제 ▶ _____

4) She must be a dentist.

　부정문 ▶ _____

**03** 두 문장의 뜻이 같도록 빈칸에 알맞은 말을 쓰시오.

1) You must turn off the computer after using it.

= You _____ _____ turn off the computer after using it.

2) They don't have to wash the dishes.

= They _____ _____ _____ wash the dishes.

3) You'd better go home now.

= You _____ better go home now.

**04** 보기와 주어진 말을 이용하여 문장을 완성하시오.

| 보기 | had better | don't have to | must |
|------|------------|---------------|------|

1) The building is on fire. We _____ _____ from the building. (escape)

2) My grandma is not sick anymore. So she _____ a doctor. (see)

3) Jack is not a good person. You _____ him. (not, meet)

05 다음 문장을 우리말로 해석하시오.

1) My mom will have to meet my homeroom teacher tomorrow.

→ _____

2) He had to follow her advice yesterday.

→ _____

3) The answer can't be wrong.

→ _____

06 우리말과 일치하도록 주어진 말을 바르게 배열하시오.

1) 그 남자는 소방수일 리 없다. (man, be, the, can't, a, firefighter)

→ _____

2) 그들은 내일 점심을 만들어야만 할 것이다. (make, tomorrow, have, they, lunch, will, to)

→ _____

3) 너는 나에게 거짓말하지 않는 것이 좋을 것이다. (not, to, better, you, lie, me, had)

→ _____

4) 우리는 오늘 교실을 청소할 필요가 없다. (have, classroom, to, we, the, clean, don't, today)

→ _____

5) 너는 수업 중에 휴대전화를 사용하면 안 된다. (class, use, you, in, your, should, cell phone, not)

→ _____

6) 해리는 그 아이들을 돌봐야만 했다. (children, had, of, to, care, Harry, the, take)

→ _____

07 주어진 말을 이용하여 다음 우리말을 영작하시오.

1) 그는 그 편지를 숨길 필요가 없다. (hide)

→ _____

2) 그녀는 휴식을 취해야만 했다. (take a rest)

→ _____

3) 그는 우리의 새로운 영어 선생님임에 틀림없다. (be)

→ _____

4) 우리는 여기에서 좌회전을 하면 안 된다. (turn left)

→ _____

**01** 다음 중 알맞은 것을 고르시오.

1) Ms Baker saw   himself | herself   in the mirror.

2)   That | It   is not easy to make friends.

3) My brothers are proud of   himself | themselves  .

4) He bought a bike and gave   them | it   to me.

5)   This | It   is very windy today.

6) We enjoyed   us | ourselves   last night.

7) I wrote a letter to   me | myself  .


**02** 다음 문장을 우리말로 해석하고 밑줄 친 it의 용법(대명사, 가주어, 비인칭주어)을 쓰시오.

1) It is cloudy and rainy in Korea.

→ _____   ( _____ )

2) I am reading *Harry Potter*. It is very interesting.

→ _____   ( _____ )

3) It is fun to ride a bike.

→ _____   ( _____ )

4) It is Wednesday today.

→ _____   ( _____ )


**03** 다음 문장을 우리말로 해석하고 밑줄 친 재귀대명사가 생략 가능하면 가능, 생략 불가능하면 불가능이라 쓰시오.

1) He took a picture of himself.

→ _____   ( _____ )

2) My mother made this pizza herself.

→ _____   ( _____ )

3) The actress killed herself.

→ _____   ( _____ )

4) They helped themselves to the food.

→ _____   ( _____ )

5) We ourselves told the fact to the students.

→ _____   ( _____ )

04 다음 문장의 **틀린** 부분에 밑줄을 긋고 바르게 고쳐 쓰시오.

1) That is difficult to solve this quiz.　　(→ ＿＿＿＿＿＿＿＿ )

2) You should take care of you.　　(→ ＿＿＿＿＿＿＿＿ )

3) The boys drew the pictures themself.　　(→ ＿＿＿ ＿＿＿ )

4) This is bright in this room.　　(→ ＿＿＿＿＿＿＿＿ )

5) I have a piano and one is in my room.　　(→ ＿＿＿＿＿＿＿＿ )

6) The car oneself was great.　　(→ ＿＿＿＿＿＿＿＿ )

05 우리말과 일치하도록 빈칸에 알맞은 말을 쓰시오.

1) 벌써 10분 전 7시이다.

→ ＿＿＿＿＿＿＿ ＿＿＿＿＿＿＿ already ten to seven.

2) 물을 마시는 것은 건강에 좋다.

→ ＿＿＿＿＿＿＿ is good for your health ＿＿＿＿＿＿＿ drink water.

3) 나의 남동생은 실수로 베었다.

→ My brother cut ＿＿＿＿＿＿＿ by mistake.

4) 그 학생들은 면접관들에게 그들 자신을 소개했다.

→ The students introduced ＿＿＿＿＿＿＿ to the interviewers.

5) 그녀는 서울에서 혼자 산다.

→ She lives in Seoul by ＿＿＿＿＿＿＿.

6) 오늘 아침은 매우 춥다.

→ ＿＿＿＿＿＿＿ ＿＿＿＿＿＿＿ very cold this morning.

06 주어진 말을 이용하여 다음 우리말을 영작하시오.

1) 그 아이들은 직접 그들의 방을 청소했다. (clean)

→ ＿＿＿＿＿＿＿＿＿＿＿＿＿＿＿＿＿

2) 나는 나 자신을 잘 표현하지 못한다. (express)

→ ＿＿＿＿＿＿＿＿＿＿＿＿＿＿＿＿＿

3) 그 학생들은 그들 자신에 관한 보고서를 썼다. (report)

→ ＿＿＿＿＿＿＿＿＿＿＿＿＿＿＿＿＿

4) 나의 집을 찾는 것은 쉽다. (it)

→ ＿＿＿＿＿＿＿＿＿＿＿＿＿＿＿＿＿

5) 여기서부터 박물관까지 2킬로미터이다. (from, to, museum)

→ ＿＿＿＿＿＿＿＿＿＿＿＿＿＿＿＿＿

**01** 다음 중 알맞은 것을 고르시오.

1) He lost a cell phone and bought a new  one ∣ it .

2) He lost a cell phone but found  one ∣ it .

3) There are two bags. One is his and  another ∣ the other  is mine.

4) I don't like the color of this shirt. Could you show me  another ∣ other ?

5) Some people like action movies and  others ∣ other  like romantic movies.

6) They know each  other ∣ another  well.

7) People have to help one  other ∣ another .

8) Each team  have ∣ has  11 players in a soccer game.

9) Every  visitors ∣ visitor  can speak Korean.

**02** 우리말과 일치하도록 빈칸에 알맞은 말을 쓰시오.

1) 나의 조부모님 두 분 모두 살아 계신다.

→ _____ of my grandparents are alive.

2) 그들 둘 다 스페인어를 할 수 없다.

→ _____ of them can speak Spanish.

3) 너희 둘 중 한 명은 집에 있어야 한다.

→ _____ of you should stay at home.

4) 두 송이 꽃이 있다. 한 송이는 장미이고 다른 한 송이는 백합이다.

→ There are two flowers. _____ is a rose and _____

_____ is a lily.

5) 많은 책들이 있다. 어떤 것은 만화책이고 다른 어떤 것은 잡지이다.

→ There are many books. _____ are comic books and _____ are

magazines.

6) 나의 동생은 장미를 좋아한다. 나는 그녀를 위해 하나 사고 싶다.

→ My sister likes roses. I would like to buy _____ for her.

7) 커피 한 잔 더 드시겠습니까?

→ Would you like _____ ___ cup of coffee?

8) 교실에 있는 소녀들은 서로서로 이야기하고 있다.

→ Many girls in the classroom are talking to _____ _____.

**03** 빈칸에 공통으로 들어갈 알맞은 말을 보기에서 골라 쓰시오.

        one         every         each         either

1) I need a new hat so I will buy _____.

    I made two e-pals. _____ lives in China and the other lives in England.

2) There are two pencils. You can choose _____ of them.

    Tim does not have a car and Mia does not, _____.

3) _____ team has a coach.

    He plays tennis _____ Saturday.

4) The boy and the girl are looking at _____ other.

    _____ of the boys brought a dog here.

**04** 밑줄 친 부분을 바르게 고쳐 쓰시오.

1) My computer doesn't work. I need to buy a new it.         (→ _____ )

2) She planted two trees. One is a pine tree and another is an apple tree. (→ _____ )

3) Every girls want to get prettier.         (→ _____ )

4) Each of the students have to study hard.         (→ _____ )

5) Neither of his grandparents can't drive.         (→ _____ )

6) Both of her sons is playing with sand.         (→ _____ )

7) Some kids are singing and other are dancing.         (→ _____ )

**05** 주어진 말을 이용하여 다음 우리말을 영작하시오.

1) 그 두 소녀는 서로 돕기를 원한다. (each other)

    → _____

2) 나의 여동생 둘 다 이 책을 읽지 않을 것이다. (neither)

    → _____

3) 나는 사과가 두 개 있다. 하나는 네 것이고 다른 하나는 나의 것이다. (other)

    → _____

4) 모든 아이들이 이 장난감을 가지고 노는 것을 좋아한다. (every, with, toy)

    → _____

**01** 다음 중 알맞은 것을 고르시오.

1) A teacher is a person   who ∣ which   teaches students at school.

2) I have a room   who ∣ which   has a lot of books.

3) I will meet the lady   whose ∣ whom   you talked about.

4) Daniel is the man   whom ∣ whose   we can trust.

5) I know the girl   who ∣ whose   father is a dentist.

6) The people   who ∣ whom   live in this castle have a party every day.


**02** 관계대명사를 사용하여 다음 두 문장을 한 문장으로 쓰시오.

1) I like the boys. They are singing on the stage.

→ _____

2) This is the boy. My sister likes him.

→ _____

3) I don't know the boy. His name is Harry.

→ _____

4) Tina will meet the man. Her sister will marry him.

→ _____


**03** 빈칸에 알맞은 관계대명사를 넣고 우리말로 해석하시오.

1) They have a daughter _____ is good at playing the piano.

→ _____

2) I know the man _____ my friend will invite.

→ _____

3) I met a woman _____ son won a gold medal.

→ _____

4) The lady _____ is drinking coffee over there is my teacher.

→ _____

5) Is this the child _____ you are looking for?

→ _____

O4 밑줄 친 부분을 바르게 고쳐 쓰시오.

1) Do you know the girl which is dancing on TV?　　　　(→ _____ )

2) Please give the book to the man who hair is white.　　(→ _____ )

3) The palace whom we visited was very large.　　　　 (→ _____ )

4) The girl whose is riding a bike is my sister　　　　　(→ _____ )

5) My brother hates the woman whom drinks a lot.　　 (→ _____ )

6) He likes girls who fingers are long and white.　　　(→ _____ )


O5 우리말과 일치하도록 주어진 말을 바르게 배열하시오.

1) 간호사는 아픈 사람들을 돌봐주는 사람이다.

(a nurse, is, who, people, takes care of, sick, a person)

→ _____

2) 브라이언은 모든 학생들이 좋아하는 선생님이다.

(a teacher, who, is, all the students, Brian, like)

→ _____

3) 나는 가족이 독일에 사는 친구 한 명이 있다.

(a friend, I, lives, whose, family, in, Germany, have)

→ _____

4) 선생님들은 항상 학교에 지각하는 학생들을 알고 있다.

(students, teachers, know, are, for, always, who, late, school)

→ _____


O6 주어진 말을 이용하여 다음 우리말을 영작하시오.

1) 의사는 아픈 사람들을 치료하는 사람이다. (treat)

→ _____

2) 이 분은 많은 책을 읽은 사람이다. (man, a lot of)

→ _____

3) 이 아이는 그가 후원하고 있는 아이이다. (support)

→ _____

4) 우리는 남편이 교수인 그 여자에 대해 얘기하는 중이다. (professor, talk about)

→ _____

5) 내가 도와주었던 그 소년은 불쌍해 보였다. (poor)

→ _____

O1  다음 중 알맞은 것을 고르시오.

1) This is the cello   whose | which   he plays every day.

2) He is driving a car   who | which   has two doors.

3) Look at the trees   whose | which   leaves turn red and yellow.

4) Can you see the woman and the cats   which | that   are in the car?

5) This is the very man   which | that   supported you.


O2  관계대명사를 사용하여 다음 두 문장을 한 문장으로 쓰시오.

1)  He has a house. It looks very large.

    → _____

2)  This is the cell phone. My mother bought it for me.

    → _____

3)  I have a computer. Its mouse looks like a real mouse.

    → _____

4)  Look at the man and his dogs. They are walking along the river.

    → _____

5) The digital camera is very expensive. I lost it a month ago.

    → _____


O3  빈칸에 알맞은 관계대명사를 넣고 우리말로 해석하시오.

1)  There are a lot of tests _____ I have to take.

    → _____

2) I have already finished the homework _____ you gave me last week.

    → _____

3) You need to know the very rules _____ we should follow.

    → _____

4) The only thing _____ I want is a bottle of water.

    → _____

5) The cat _____ fur is soft and white is sleeping on my leg.

    → _____

## 04 밑줄 친 부분을 바르게 고쳐 쓰시오.

1) You should return the book whose I lent you.  (→ _____ )

2) Jason will give you everything which you want.  (→ _____ )

3) I have a class who begins at 8:30.  (→ _____ )

4) This is the coffee shop which owner is my uncle.  (→ _____ )

5) He has a car which color is gray.  (→ _____ )

6) The girl and her puppy which are playing together look happy.  (→ _____ )

## 05 우리말과 일치하도록 주어진 말을 바르게 배열하시오.

1) 이것은 내가 이해하지 못한 책이다.

(don't, that, is, the book, this, I, understand)

→ _____

2) 저에게 서랍이 많은 책상을 보여주세요.

(a lot of, which, me, the desk, please show, has, drawers)

→ _____

3) 나는 너에게 사람들이 많이 읽은 소설을 빌려줄 것이다.

(people, lend, will, you, which, the novel, read, I, a lot)

→ _____

4) 그는 날개가 빨간색인 잠자리를 보고 있다.

(wings, is, the dragonfly, looking, at, he, are, whose, red)

→ _____

5) 이것은 내가 지금까지 먹어본 중 가장 맛이 좋은 음식이다.

(is, the most, this, have, delicious, food, that, ever, I, eaten)

→ _____

## 06 주어진 말을 이용하여 다음 우리말을 영작하시오.

1) 그녀는 내가 지난 일요일에 고친 자전거를 타고 있다. (fix)

→ _____

2) 나는 어젯밤에 본 영화가 맘에 든다. (watch)

→ _____

3) 나는 표지가 플라스틱인 그 공책이 마음에 든다. (plastic, cover)

→ _____

4) 그는 북극에 도착한 최초의 사람이다. (the North Pole, reach)

→ _____

**01** 다음 중 알맞은 것을 고르시오.

1) This is the house in   which | what | that   Vincent Van Gogh lived.

2) He is the boy with   which | that | whom   I played soccer.

3) Please ask me   which | what | that   you don't know.

4) Please put down the pencil with   which | what | that   you wrote.

**02** 다음 문장을 우리말로 해석하시오.

1) You have to remember what you learn today.

  → _____

2) This is what I want to buy for you.

  → _____

3) What my boss said is not true.

  → _____

4) Do you know the boy to whom Sora is talking?

  → _____

5) The chair on which we will sit looks very comfortable.

  → _____

**03** 다음 문장에서 생략할 수 있는 부분에 밑줄을 그으시오.

1) I want to marry a man whom many people respect.

2) My brother wants to buy the computer which I recommend.

3) The girl who is playing the piano is my sister.

4) My sister loves the doll which is made of glass.

**04** 두 문장의 뜻이 같도록 빈칸에 알맞은 말을 쓰시오.

1) I heard the news _____ they were talking about.

  = I heard the news _____ _____ they were talking.

2) I need a friend _____ I live with.

  = I need a friend _____ _____ I live.

3) We will visit the bank _____ my father works at.

  = We will visit the bank _____ _____ my father works.

○5 생략된 관계대명사를 알맞은 곳에 넣어 문장을 다시 쓰시오.

1) This is the boy you should help.

→ _____

2) The picture Karen took in Canada was wonderful.

→ _____

3) My father is the man driving a truck over there.

→ _____

4) This is the most difficult question I have ever solved.

→ _____


○6 우리말과 일치하도록 주어진 말을 바르게 배열하시오.

1) 그는 항상 내가 듣고 싶지 않는 것을 말한다.

(don't, says, always, I, to, he, want, what, hear)

→ _____

2) 나의 손 안에 있는 것은 호두이다.

(my, is, in, is, hand, what, a walnut)

→ _____

3) 너의 관심은 너의 아들이 필요로 하는 것이다.

(your, what, care, is, son, your, needs)

→ _____

4) 한 부유한 사람이 네가 그린 그림을 사기를 원한다.

(a rich man, to, buy, you, the picture, wants, painted)

→ _____

5) 이 공장에서 일하는 사람들은 부지런해 보인다.

(diligent, working, who, are, in, factory, this, the people, look)

→ _____


○7 주어진 말을 이용하여 다음 우리말을 영작하시오.

1) 나의 여동생은 내가 갖고 있는 것을 항상 원한다. (always)

→ _____

2) 네가 배우려고 노력하는 것이 중요하다. (important)

→ _____

3) 나는 나의 남동생이 관심 있어 하는 장난감을 사 주었다. (be interested in)

→ _____

○1 다음 중 알맞은 것을 고르시오.

1) I can't understand the reason   when | why   you changed your mind.

2) My daughter is waiting for the day   when | where   school starts.

3) I want to go to a hotel   when | where   the bathrooms are large.

4) 2002 is the year   when | where   the World Cup was held in Korea.

5) Tell me   the way how | how   you could succeed in your work.

6) Bill told me the reason   why | how   he gave up smoking.

7) She misses the town   when | where   she stayed last year.


○2 관계부사를 사용하여 다음 두 문장을 한 문장으로 쓰시오.

1) I like the city. Mozart lived there.

→ _____

2) We will meet in the hotel. My sister got married in the hotel.

→ _____

3) Winter is the season. We can ski and skate in the season.

→ _____

4) Tell me the reason. She didn't take a test for the reason.

→ _____

5) I know the way. He made this program that way.

→ _____


○3 빈칸에 알맞은 관계부사를 넣고 우리말로 해석하시오.

1) I know the reason _____ he didn't come back.

→ _____

2) I won't forget the day _____ I first met you.

→ _____

3) He went into the room _____ there was nothing.

→ _____

4) This is _____ he solved the problem.

→ _____

○4 밑줄 친 부분을 바르게 고쳐 쓰시오.

1) This is the apartment when I lived five years ago.     (→ _____ )

2) I don't know the way how my mom cooks spaghetti.     (→ _____ )

3) He will ask me the reason when she bought the bag.     (→ _____ )

4) 2012 is the year where my nephew was born.     (→ _____ )

5) There are many countries which I want to take a trip.     (→ _____ )

6) Winter is the season why it snows a lot.     (→ _____ )

○5 우리말과 일치하도록 주어진 말을 바르게 배열하시오.

1) 너는 우리가 소풍 갔던 공원을 기억하니?

(you, the park, do, remember, we, went, where, on a picnic)

→ _____

2) 네가 학교에 지각한 이유를 말해라.

(me, why, the reason, late, you, were, for, tell, school)

→ _____

3) 그는 나무와 꽃이 많은 숲을 걷는 것을 좋아한다.

(a lot of, walk, are, where, in the forest, he, there, likes, trees and flowers, to)

→ _____

4) 여름은 사람들이 바다에서 수영할 수 있는 계절이다.

(is, swim, summer, the season, people, can, in, when, the sea)

→ _____

5) 나는 그녀가 영어를 유창하게 말하는 것을 배웠던 방법을 알고 싶다.

(I, to, fluently, know, she, English, learned, speak, the way, to, want)

→ _____

○6 주어진 말을 이용하여 다음 우리말을 영작하시오.

1) 도서관은 우리가 책을 빌릴 수 있는 곳이다. (library, borrow)

→ _____

2) 1월 5일은 10년 전에 내가 한국에 온 날이다. (January)

→ _____

3) 나는 그가 비행기를 놓친 이유를 모른다. (miss)

→ _____

**O1** 밑줄 친 부분을 바르게 고쳐 쓰시오.

1) Sally has <u>much</u> friends.    (→ _____ )

2) He drank <u>a few</u> milk.    (→ _____ )

3) We gave up <u>it</u>.    (→ _____ )

4) They don't drink <u>some</u> juice.    (→ _____ )

5) Harry has <u>a great deal</u> of toys.    (→ _____ )

6) My sister has <u>any</u> books.    (→ _____ )

**O2** 주어진 말을 알맞은 위치에 넣어 문장을 다시 쓰시오.

1) You can join our club. (always)

   → _____

2) The machine is out of order. (sometimes)

   → _____

3) Suzie takes a walk with her sister. (usually)

   → _____

**O3** 우리말과 일치하도록 빈칸에 알맞은 말을 보기에서 골라 쓰시오.

> **보기**    a number of    a few    a little    few    little    a great deal of

1) 그는 운동을 상당히 많이 한다.

   → He does _____ exercise.

2) 많은 학생들이 교실에 있다.

   → There are _____ students in the classroom.

3) 나는 연필 몇 개를 가지고 있다.

   → I have _____ pencils.

4) 그곳에는 사람이 거의 살지 않았다.

   → _____ people lived there.

5) 약간의 물이 그들을 살렸다.

   → _____ water saved them.

6) 그녀는 돈이 거의 없다.

   → She has _____ money.

○4 **다음 문장을 우리말로 해석하시오.**

1) He put the shirt on.

→ _____

2) They know a few baseball players.

→ _____

3) I drink little coffee.

→ _____

4) She added a little salt to the soup.

→ _____


○5 **우리말과 일치하도록 주어진 말을 바르게 배열하시오.**

1) 너는 항상 우리와 같이 영어 공부를 할 수 있다.

(always, English, you, study, with, us, can)

→ _____

2) 해리와 그의 친구들은 그것을 어린이들을 위해 설립했다.

(friends, up, children, Harry, for, it, and, set, his)

→ _____

3) 내 친구는 나에게 절대 화내지 않는다.

(with, is, me, angry, my, never, friend)

→ _____

4) 그는 자주 그의 부모님과 여행을 떠난다.

(parents, often, he, with, travels, his)

→ _____


○6 **주어진 말을 이용하여 다음 우리말을 영작하시오.**

1) 케이트(Kate)는 그녀의 안경을 벗었다. (take off, glasses)

→ _____

2) 제임스(James)는 가끔 일요일에 도서관에 간다. (sometimes)

→ _____

3) 그는 친구가 거의 없다. (have)

→ _____

4) 너는 연필을 가지고 있니? (have)

→ _____

○1 주어진 단어의 원급, 비교급, 최상급을 이용하여 다음 문장을 완성하시오.

1) They are the _____ players in the club.  (good)

2) The situation is _____ than I thought.  (bad)

3) He is the _____ man in the world.  (lucky)

4) We have much _____ money than you.  (much)

5) This is the _____ question in the book.  (important)

6) He is not as _____ as her.  (creative)

7) She is _____ than my sister.  (thin)

8) Your puppy is the _____ of all the pets.  (cute)


○2 밑줄 친 부분을 바르게 고쳐 쓰시오.

1) This is an ugliest coat in the store.          (→ _____ )

2) This room is very worse than that one.          (→ _____ )

3) This photo is clearest than that one.          (→ _____ )

4) He is the happier boy in my class.          (→ _____ )

5) This wall is not as higher as that one.          (→ _____ )

6) This novel is much most romantic than that one.          (→ _____ )

7) She is the cleverer of all the students.          (→ _____ )


○3 두 문장의 뜻이 같도록 빈칸에 알맞은 말을 쓰시오.

1) This book is not as thick as that one.

 → That book is _____ _____ this one.

2) James is 15 years old. Paul is 15 years old, too.

 → James is _____ _____ _____ Paul.

3) Kate is lighter than Suzie.

 → Suzie is _____ _____ Kate.

4) Bag A is 10,000 won, Bag B is 10,000 won, and Bag C is 20,000 won.

 → Bag A is _____ _____ Bag C.

 → Bag C is _____ _____ of all.

5) Charles is not as tall as Tommy.

 → Charles is _____ _____ Tommy.

○4 **다음 문장을 우리말로 해석하시오.**

1) This classroom is not as tidy as that one.

→ _____

2) Winter is the coldest of all seasons.

→ _____

3) Jane is much more popular than Susan.

→ _____

4) This is the most dangerous place in the world.

→ _____


○5 **우리말과 일치하도록 주어진 말을 바르게 배열하시오.**

1) 이것은 이 나라에서 가장 아름다운 건물이다.  (country, this, most, is, the, in, beautiful, the, building)

→ _____

2) 제리는 톰보다 훨씬 더 잘생겼다.  (than, is, much, Jerry, handsome, Tom, more)

→ _____

3) 이 도시는 저 도시만큼 깨끗하다.  (one, as, this, as, city, is, clean, that)

→ _____

4) 이 학생은 모든 학생들 중 가장 약하다.  (is, the, of, student, all, weakest, this)

→ _____

5) 이 문제는 저 문제만큼 쉽지 않다.  (as, one, this, is, problem, not, easy, that, as)

→ _____


○6 **주어진 말을 이용하여 다음 우리말을 영작하시오.**

1) 제니퍼(Jennifer)는 수잔(Susan)만큼 참을성이 있지 않다.  (patient)

→ _____

2) 101호는 이 호텔에서 가장 작은 방이다.  (Room 101, tiny)

→ _____

3) 이 소파는 저 소파보다 훨씬 더 편안하다.  (even, comfortable)

→ _____

4) 과학은 수학만큼 어렵다.  (science, mathematics)

→ _____

**01** 다음 중 알맞은 것을 고르시오.

1) Kate is one of the prettiest   girls | girl   in my class.

2) He is getting   more careful and more careful | more and more careful  .

3) This dog is three times as   heavier than | heavy as   that dog.

4) The   quickest | quicker  , the   best | better  .

5) Who is   honest | more honest  , Bill or Hillary?

6) The road is becoming   wide and wide | wider and wider  .

7) This cat is three times   as fat as | fatter   than that one.

**02** 주어진 말을 알맞은 형태로 바꾸어 빈칸에 쓰시오.

1) The sky is getting _____ and _____. (dark)

2) The _____ a comic book is, the _____ it is.  (funny, popular)

3) Which is _____, a science book or a history book?  (exciting)

4) This is one of the _____ _____ in the world.  (old, building)

5) This cake is twice as _____ as that one.  (soft)

**03** 밑줄 친 부분을 바르게 고쳐 쓰시오.

1) Suzie is one of the bright students in my school.　　　(→ _____ )

2) The cold it is, the more we stay at home.　　　(→ _____ )

3) He is getting smart and smart.　　　(→ _____ )

4) Who is generous, James or Paul?　　　(→ _____ )

5) This street is four times narrow than that one.　　　(→ _____ )

**04** 다음 문장을 우리말로 해석하시오.

1) The older you get, the wiser you will be.

　→ _____

2) The problem is becoming more and more important.

　→ _____

3) This country is three times as rich as that one.

　→ _____

05 우리말과 일치하도록 빈칸에 알맞은 말을 쓰시오.

1) 방이 작을수록 더 싸다.
The _____ a room is, the _____ it is.

2) 쿠웨이트는 이 세상에서 가장 더운 나라들 중 하나이다.
Kuwait is one of the _____ _____ in the world.

3) 사과와 바나나 중에서 어느 것이 더 맛있니?
Which is _____ _____, an apple or a banana?

4) 그 학생은 점점 부지런해지고 있다.
The student is becoming _____ _____ _____ diligent.

06 우리말과 일치하도록 주어진 말을 바르게 배열하시오.

1) 너는 천천히 먹을수록 더 건강해질 것이다. (be, the, will, you, the, eat, you, slower, healthier)
→ _____

2) 우리의 생활이 점점 더 편리해지고 있다. (more, our, is, and, convenient, life, more, becoming)
→ _____

3) 이 새는 저 새보다 세 배 더 높이 난다. (one, as, this, three, bird, high, that, flies, as, times)
→ _____

4) 가위와 칼 중에서 어느 것이 더 유용하니? (scissors, useful, or, is, a, which, cutter, more)
→ _____

07 주어진 말을 이용하여 다음 우리말을 영작하시오.

1) 비쌀수록 더 좋다. (expensive)
→ _____

2) 그 강은 점점 더 깊어진다. (get)
→ _____

3) 캐빈(Kevin)과 에이미(Amy) 중 누가 더 긴장하니? (nervous)
→ _____

4) 그는 한국에서 가장 재능 있는 화가들 중 한 명이다. (talented, painter)
→ _____

5) 이 탁자는 저 탁자보다 세 배 더 낮다. (low)
→ _____

**01** 밑줄 친 부분에 해당하는 문장 요소를 괄호 안에 쓰시오.

1) He made his daughter a movie star. (→ _____ )

2) She made her son a cheese sandwich. (→ _____ )

3) There are some pears in the box. (→ _____ )

4) The pizza on the table looks tasty. (→ _____ )

5) He bought his brother some juice. (→ _____ )

6) She lent her notebook to Mary. (→ _____ )

7) Sweating makes our bodies cool. (→ _____ )

**02** 보기와 같이 다음 문장의 밑줄 친 부분을 문장 요소로 구분하여 표시하시오.

> 보기
>
> He drives a car carefully.
> 주어  동사   목적어

1) There is some food in the refrigerator.

2) The workers are building the bridge.

3) We sent poor babies gloves.

4) We made a snowman quickly.

5) My sister became a famous actress.

6) She always keeps her hands and feet warm.

**03** 다음 중 알맞은 것을 고르시오.

1) This lemon tastes  sour | sourly .

2) I will show  he | him | his  my necklace.

3) The girl looks  beautiful | beautifully | beauty .

4) This tea does not taste  sweet | sweetly | sweetness .

5) Reading gives us  happy | happily | happiness .

6) The movie makes people  sad | sadly | sadness .

**04** 밑줄 친 부분에 유의하여 다음 문장을 우리말로 해석하시오.

1) The seller made children cotton candy.

→ _____

2) Jiho's parents made their daughter a member of a girl group.

→ _____

3) He found the book easy.

→ _____

4) He found the book easily.

→ _____

**05** 우리말과 일치하도록 주어진 말을 바르게 배열하시오.

1) 은행에는 많은 사람들이 있었다.

(there, of, people, in, were, a lot, the bank)

→ _____

2) 한 노동자가 2주 전에 그 사장에게 편지를 썼다.

(wrote, weeks, a letter, two, a worker, the boss, ago)

→ _____

3) 이 식당의 음식은 아주 맛이 좋다.

(restaurant, in, tastes, very, this, the food, good)

→ _____

4) 우리는 비밀리에 그 컴퓨터를 주말마다 사용했다.

(the computer, secretly, every, we, weekend, used)

→ _____

**06** 주어진 말을 이용하여 다음 우리말을 영작하시오.

1) 그는 일 년 전에 빵집에서 일했다. (at a bakery)

→ _____

2) 그녀는 이 문제를 쉽게 풀었다. (question)

→ _____

3) 나의 삼촌은 매주 나에게 10,000원을 준다. (every week)

→ _____

4) 그 오래된 화장실은 이상한 냄새가 난다. (toilet)

→ _____

**O1** 다음 중 알맞은 것을 고르시오.

1) The plants smell   fresh ǀ freshly ǀ freshness  .

2) Her skin feels really   smooth ǀ smoothly  .

3) The movie, *Transformers*, looks   wonderful ǀ wonderfully  .

4) My friends talked to each other   quietly ǀ quiet ǀ quietness  .

5) Everyone enjoyed   free ǀ freedom ǀ freely   and peace.

6) The girl dances   beautiful ǀ beautifully ǀ beauty  .

7) We visited   they ǀ their ǀ them   last Sunday.

8) My mother saw   she ǀ his ǀ herself   in the mirror.

**O2** 다음 문장의 형식을 쓰고 밑줄 친 말에 유의하여 우리말로 해석하시오.

1) My mother will taste the chicken soup.

→ _____

2) The chicken soup tastes delicious.

→ _____

3) You may smell this fruit.

→ _____

4) This fruit smells sweet.

→ _____

5) The weather got colder and colder.

→ _____

6) He got a gift from his girlfriend.

→ _____

**O3** 다음 문장의 틀린 부분에 밑줄을 긋고 바르게 고쳐 쓰시오.

1) This blanket feels so softly.        (→ _____ )

2) The potato pizza tastes very well.        (→ _____ )

3) Shirley always gets angrily.        (→ _____ )

4) Her family looks health.        (→ _____ )

5) We know their very well.        (→ _____ )

6) Mina always smiles happy.        (→ _____ )

○4 우리말과 일치하도록 주어진 말을 바르게 배열하시오.

1) 그녀는 작년에 서울대학교를 졸업했다. (last, Seoul National University, she, graduated from, year)

→ _____

2) 내 조카는 점점 더 게을러졌다. (is, growing, lazier, nephew, my, and, lazier)

→ _____

3) 내 친구는 내년에 수학선생님이 될 것이다. (next, friend, will, teacher, my, become, a, math, year)

→ _____

4) 탁자 위에 치즈 한 조각이 있다. (a piece, of, cheese, on, is, there, the table)

→ _____

5) 그녀는 동굴 안으로 그녀의 친구들을 따라갔다. (friends, she, into, followed, her, the cave)

→ _____

6) 경찰들이 자동차 아래에서 그 고양이를 발견했다. (the car, the police, under, found, the cat)

→ _____

7) 이 이야기는 나에게 흥미롭게 들린다. (this, interesting, to, sounds, me, story)

→ _____

○5 주어진 말을 이용하여 다음 우리말을 영작하시오.

1) 그녀의 아들은 점점 힘이 세졌다. (get)

→ _____

2) 그의 목소리는 이상하게 들린다. (voice)

→ _____

3) 너는 졸려 보인다. (sleepy)

→ _____

4) 나의 오빠는 1년 전에는 군인이었다. (soldier)

→ _____

5) 너는 도서관에서 책을 빌릴 수 있다. (can, borrow)

→ _____

6) 케이트(Kate)는 그의 질문에 친절하게 대답했다. (kindly)

→ _____

**01** 두 문장의 뜻이 같도록 빈칸에 알맞은 말을 쓰시오.

1) I will give you a second chance.

= I will give a second chance _____.

2) She made her mom spaghetti.

= She made spaghetti _____.

3) My mom bought me a suitcase.

= My mom _____.

4) Students ask their teacher questions.

= Students _____.

5) She lent her brother her cell phone.

= _____

6) She wrote Christmas cards to her parents.

= _____


**02** 다음 중 알맞은 것을 고르시오.

1) Mr. Jang taught   she ǀ her ǀ hers   Chinese.

2) Karen showed her pictures   to ǀ for ǀ of   me.

3) May I ask a favor   to ǀ for ǀ of   you?

4) The grandmother told a strange story   to Kelly ǀ for Kelly ǀ Kelly .

5) People called the girl   to Sora ǀ for Sora ǀ Sora .

6) The story made us   sad ǀ sadness ǀ sadly .

7) We should keep our body   health ǀ healthy ǀ healthily .

8) Brian will   send ǀ buy   a toy car for his son.


**03** 다음 문장의 <u>틀린</u> 부분에 밑줄을 긋고 바르게 고쳐 쓰시오.

1) We elected Mr. Kim to president.     (→ _____ )

2) I sent an email for my classmates.     (→ _____ )

3) We will name Yuri our baby.     (→ _____ )

4) Please buy some bread to me.     (→ _____ )

5) Singing makes me happily.     (→ _____ )

6) He always keeps his room dirtily.     (→ _____ )

O4 우리말과 일치하도록 주어진 말을 바르게 배열하시오.

1) 경찰들은 그 집이 비어있다는 것을 알았다.
(the police, the house, found, empty)

→ _____

2) 그 회사는 항상 근로자들에게 크리스마스 보너스를 준다.
(gives, workers, the company, always, a Christmas bonus)

→ _____

3) 많은 부모들은 그들의 아들과 딸들을 천재라고 생각한다.
(their sons, parents, and, daughters, think, many, geniuses)

→ _____

4) 제발 그 별명으로 나를 부르지 마세요.
(please, call, me, that, don't, nickname)

→ _____

5) 아버지는 지난 주말에 나에게 바지 한 벌을 사 주셨다.
(dad, pants, last, bought, me, of, a pair, weekend)

→ _____

6) 나는 매일 아침 부모님에게 바나나 주스를 만들어 드린다.
(I, make, for, my parents, every, banana juice, morning)

→ _____


O5 주어진 말을 이용하여 다음 우리말을 영작하시오.

1) 나는 나의 어머니를 화나게 했다. (make)

→ _____

2) 우리는 그 아이들에게 빵과 물을 사 주었다. (buy)

→ _____

→ _____

3) 그는 그녀가 현명하다는 것을 알았다. (find)

→ _____

4) 우리는 그를 지도자로 선출했다. (elect, leader)

→ _____

5) 우리는 그에게 약간의 시간을 주었다.

→ _____

→ _____

**01** to부정사에 밑줄을 긋고 무슨 역할인지 보기에서 골라 쓰시오.

　　　　　　 주어　　　　　 목적어　　　　　 보어

1) He is planning to build a house.　　　　( _____ )

2) It is nice to help people.　　　　　　　 ( _____ )

3) His plan is to go to London next year.　( _____ )

4) She wants to plant some flowers.　　　 ( _____ )

5) Her dream is to become a dentist.　　　( _____ )

6) To make a homepage is interesting.　　 ( _____ )

**02** 다음 문장의 **틀린** 부분에 밑줄을 긋고 바르게 고쳐 쓰시오.

1) I asked him how to the bottle open.　　( → _____ )

2) This is simple to paint the room.　　　 ( → _____ )

3) They know when going home.　　　　 ( → _____ )

4) He decided to not buy a new car.　　　( → _____ )

5) We will show him where stay tonight.　( → _____ )

6) She hoped have a party.　　　　　　　( → _____ )

7) To making a study plan is good for you.　( → _____ )

**03** 두 문장의 의미가 같도록 빈칸에 알맞은 말을 쓰시오.

1) She didn't know what to cook for dinner.

= She didn't know _____ _____ _____
_____ for dinner.

2) She will remember when to see a doctor.

= She will remember _____ _____ _____
_____ a doctor.

3) I want to know how to fix the bike.

= I want to know _____ _____ _____
_____ the bike.

4) Do they know where to park their car?

= Do they know _____ _____ _____
_____ their car?

04 다음 문장을 우리말로 해석하시오.

1) I decided not to eat ice cream too much.

→ _____

2) He asked me where to buy a suit.

→ _____

3) Her hobby is to play badminton with her friend.

→ _____

4) They want to know when to visit the Science Museum.

→ _____


05 우리말과 일치하도록 주어진 말을 바르게 배열하시오.

1) 수잔은 그에게 어떻게 문제를 해결하는지 가르쳐주었다.

(the problem, him, solve, how, Susan, to, taught)

→ _____

2) 나는 영어 시험에 떨어지기를 원하지 않는다.

(fail, I, don't, the English test, to, want)

→ _____

3) 우리는 그것을 언제 끝내야 하는지 모른다.

(we, it, don't, we, when, should, know, finish)

→ _____


06 주어진 말을 이용하여 다음 우리말을 영작하시오.

1) 친구와 싸우는 것은 좋지 않다.  (fight with)

→ _____

2) 우리는 세계일주 여행을 계획하고 있다.  (around the world)

→ _____

3) 그녀는 그 지도를 어떻게 읽는지 안다.  (read the map)

→ _____

4) 나의 목표는 매일 줄넘기를 하는 것이다.  (goal, jump rope)

→ _____

5) 그들은 무엇을 먹을지 결정했다.  (decide)

→ _____

**01** to부정사에 밑줄을 긋고 무슨 역할인지 보기에서 골라 쓰시오.

> [보기]  형용사    부사(목적)    부사(감정의 원인)    부사(결과)    부사(형용사 수식)

1) She has someone to trust.                    ( _____ )
2) I went to the library to borrow some books.  ( _____ )
3) He is excited to watch a baseball game.      ( _____ )
4) There are a lot of benches to sit on.        ( _____ )
5) She grew up to become a famous painter.      ( _____ )
6) The question is difficult to answer.         ( _____ )
7) It is time to go to school.                  ( _____ )

**02** 다음 문장의 틀린 부분에 밑줄을 긋고 바르게 고쳐 쓰시오.

1) She had the radio to listen.          (→ _____ )
2) We are glad hear the news.            (→ _____ )
3) Suzie bought the piano to play with.  (→ _____ )
4) He grew up becoming an actor.         (→ _____ )
5) Mom went to the market buying apples. (→ _____ )
6) The river is clean swim in.           (→ _____ )
7) He has a pen to write.                (→ _____ )
8) I ran fast in order catch the bus.    (→ _____ )

**03** 두 문장의 의미가 같도록 빈칸에 알맞은 말을 쓰시오.

1) She wants to study in Canada so she is learning English.

= She is learning English _____ _____ in Canada.

2) He won the race so he was happy.

= He was happy _____ _____ the race.

3) I went to bed late because I had to finish my homework.

= I went to bed late in order _____ _____ my homework.

4) They are sad because they lost their bikes.

= They are sad _____ _____ their bikes.

○4 다음 문장을 우리말로 해석하시오.

1) He grew up to become a pianist.

→ _____

2) She was excited to win first prize.

→ _____

3) We turned on the TV in order to watch the Olympic Games.

→ _____


○5 우리말과 일치하도록 주어진 말을 바르게 배열하시오.

1) 내 생일을 축하하기 위하여 나는 파티를 열 것이다.

(a party, I, celebrate, in, will, order, my birthday, have, to)

→ _____

2) 그들은 살 새로운 집을 사기를 원한다.

(to, a new house, buy, they, live, want, in, to)

→ _____

3) 그는 입학시험에 떨어져서 충격을 받았다.

(shocked, the entrance exam, to, was, he, fail)

→ _____

4) 그녀는 백 살까지 살았다.

(to, 100 years old, lived, she, be)

→ _____


○6 주어진 말을 이용하여 다음 우리말을 영작하시오.

1) 그는 샌드위치를 만들기 위하여 빵을 조금 샀다. (sandwich)

→ _____

2) 나는 옛날 일기장을 찾아서 반가웠다. (diary)

→ _____

3) 그 사진기는 사용하기 쉽다. (use)

→ _____

4) 그녀는 자라서 영어선생님이 되었다. (become)

→ _____

5) 그들은 가지고 놀 장난감을 샀다. (toy)

→ _____

**○1** 다음 중 알맞은 것을 고르시오.

1) It is impossible   for | of   me to assemble a computer.

2) It was silly   for | of   her not to talk to her friends.

3) It is easy   for | of   them to climb Mt. Halla.

4) It was kind   for | of   him to pick us up from the airport.

**○2** 다음 문장의 <u>틀린</u> 부분에 밑줄을 긋고 바르게 고쳐 쓰시오.

1) It was not easy them to study hard.          (→ _____ )

2) It is difficult of her to stay up late.          (→ _____ )

3) This is dangerous to walk on the ice.          (→ _____ )

4) It is relaxing for me walk along the river.          (→ _____ )

5) It was stupid of they to run away.          (→ _____ )

**○3** 두 문장의 의미가 같도록 빈칸에 알맞은 말을 쓰시오.

1) To go skiing with friends will be exciting.

= _____ _____ _____ _____ to go skiing with friends.

2) To make a snowman with my family was fun.

= _____ _____ _____ to make a snowman with my family.

3) To speak a lot of languages is useful.

= _____ _____ _____ to speak a lot of languages.

**○4** 우리말과 일치하도록 빈칸에 알맞은 말을 쓰시오.

1) 그들이 부모님 말씀을 잘 듣는 것은 현명하다.

→ It is _____ _____ _____ to listen to their parents.

2) 우리가 그 소문을 믿는 것은 어리석다.

→ It is _____ _____ _____ to believe the rumor.

3) 그녀가 아이들을 돌보는 것은 쉽지 않았다.

→ It was not _____ _____ _____ to take care of the children.

○5 **다음 문장을 우리말로 해석하시오.**

1) It was wise of her to call an ambulance.

→ _____

2) It is not difficult for him to design a house.

→ _____

3) It was silly of them to make fun of him.

→ _____

4) It is important for us not to bother others.

→ _____


○6 **우리말과 일치하도록 주어진 말을 바르게 배열하시오.**

1) 중요한 것을 기억하는 것이 필요하다.

(things, to, important, is, it, remember, necessary)

→ _____

2) 그가 그 병들을 재활용하는 것은 좋았다.

(the bottles, it, to, him, was, of, nice, recycle)

→ _____

3) 그녀가 우리에게 길을 알려준 것은 친절했다.

(of, was, the way, kind, show, her, us, it, to)

→ _____

4) 내가 한강을 수영하여 건너는 것은 불가능하다.

(the Han river, me, is, to, it, for, across, impossible, swim)

→ _____


○7 **주어진 말을 이용하여 다음 우리말을 영작하시오.**

1) 그녀가 시간을 낭비하는 것은 어리석었다. (foolish, waste)

→ It _____.

2) 그가 기타를 치는 것은 어렵지 않다. (the guitar)

→ It _____.

3) 그들이 그것을 하는 것은 현명했다. (wise)

→ It _____.

4) 그가 중국어를 배우는 것은 쉬웠다. (Chinese)

→ It _____.

**01** 다음 문장의 <u>틀린</u> 부분에 밑줄을 긋고 바르게 고쳐 쓰시오.

1) She had him to wash the dishes.      (→ _____ )

2) He asked me joining the swimming club.      (→ _____ )

3) I felt someone touched me.      (→ _____ )

4) We made her writing an English essay.      (→ _____ )

5) She told him helping us.      (→ _____ )

6) They saw her to sing in the contest.      (→ _____ )

7) Let me telling you something.      (→ _____ )

8) Mom wants me studying harder.      (→ _____ )


**02** 우리말과 일치하도록 보기에서 알맞은 단어를 골라 빈칸에 알맞은 형태로 쓰시오.

| 보기 | escape | laugh | walk | go |
|---|---|---|---|---|
| | take | burn | clear | buy |

1) 그 여자아이는 어머니에게 새로운 책가방을 사달라고 요청했다.

     → The girl asked her mom _____ a new school bag for her.

2) 나는 그가 길을 걸어가는 것을 보았다.

     → I saw him _____ down the street.

3) 그린 씨는 그들에게 길에서 눈을 치우도록 시켰다.

     → Mr. Green made them _____ the road of snow.

4) 그는 그녀가 휴식을 갖기를 원한다.

     → He wants her _____ a rest.

5) 우리는 그가 크게 웃는 것을 들었다.

     → We heard him _____ loudly.

6) 소방관은 사람들에게 건물을 빠져나가라고 말했다.

     → The firefighter told people _____ from the building.

7) 선생님은 학생들을 집에 가게 했다.

     → The teacher let the students _____ home.

8) 그는 빵이 타는 냄새를 맡았다.

     → He smelled the bread _____ .

03 다음 문장을 우리말로 해석하시오.

1) She had us clean the windows.

→ _____

2) We heard them shouting at him.

→ _____

3) The police officer made the thief fall down.

→ _____

4) The photographer told us to smile together.

→ _____


04 우리말과 일치하도록 주어진 말을 바르게 배열하시오.

1) 그는 그의 친구들이 그와 축구를 같이하기를 바란다.

(football, with, he, play, wants, to, his friends, him)

→ _____

2) 담임선생님은 우리에게 영어일기를 쓰도록 시켰다.

(an, us, keep, teacher, diary, homeroom, English, had, our)

→ _____

3) 그들은 그녀가 그들을 위해 기도하는 것을 경청했다.

(them, praying, to, they, her, listened, for)

→ _____

4) 우리는 그들이 몇 그루의 사과나무를 심게 만들 것이다.

(apple trees, them, we, some, make, plant, will)

→ _____

5) 선생님은 학생이 음악실에 들어오도록 허락했다.

(the student, to, the teacher, come, the music room, let)

→ _____


05 주어진 말을 이용하여 다음 우리말을 영작하시오.

1) 우리는 그가 소파에서 자고 있는 것을 보았다. (see)

→ _____

2) 나의 어머니는 우리가 집안일을 돕게 만들었다. (make, household chores)

→ _____

3) 그는 그들에게 최선을 다하라고 요청했다. (ask, do one's best)

→ _____

**01** 동명사에 밑줄을 긋고 무슨 역할을 하는지 보기에서 골라 쓰시오.

> 보기    주어    동사의 목적어    보어    전치사의 목적어

1) Her job is training dogs.                    ( _____ )
2) Susan enjoys listening to classical music.   ( _____ )
3) His wife is good at baking bread.            ( _____ )
4) Speaking English is not difficult.           ( _____ )
5) They will avoid meeting their enemies.       ( _____ )
6) She is proud of being a musician.            ( _____ )
7) His hobby is flying model airplanes.         ( _____ )
8) Watching a baseball game is exciting.        ( _____ )

**02** 다음 문장의 <u>틀린</u> 부분에 밑줄을 긋고 바르게 고쳐 쓰시오.

1) They are thinking about go to Jejudo.        (→ _____ )
2) Suzie is afraid of not get a job.            (→ _____ )
3) Do you mind close the door?                  (→ _____ )
4) Don't eating vegetables is bad for your health.  (→ _____ )

**03** 우리말과 일치하도록 빈칸에 알맞은 단어를 보기에서 골라 알맞은 형태로 바꿔 쓰시오.

> 보기    watch    make    advertise    keep    bite

1) 약속을 지키는 것이 중요하다.
   → _____ a promise is important.

2) 그들의 임무는 이 제품을 광고하는 것이다.
   → Their mission is _____ the product.

3) 그는 손톱을 깨무는 것을 그만두었다.
   → He gave up _____ his nails.

4) 나는 공포영화를 보는 것이 무섭다.
   → I am scared of _____ a horror movie.

5) 결정을 빨리 하지 않는 것이 우리에게 좋다.
   → _____ _____ a decision quickly is good for us.

O4 다음 문장을 우리말로 해석하시오.

1) Not going to bed early is bad for your health.

→ _____

2) She finished chatting on the phone with her friend.

→ _____

3) Your problem is having fast food too much.

→ _____

4) He was shocked at not passing the exam.

→ _____

O5 우리말과 일치하도록 주어진 말을 바르게 배열하시오.

1) 빨간 신호등에서 길을 건너지 않는 것이 규칙이다.

(the street, not, a rule, crossing, the red light, is, at)

→ _____

2) 그녀는 매일 피아노를 연습하는 데 싫증이 난다.

(the piano, she, of, is, every day, practicing, tired)

→ _____

3) 그의 직업은 팝송을 작곡하는 것이다.

(is, pop songs, job, composing, his)

→ _____

4) 그는 그 게임에 이기지 못해서 화가 났다.

(not, the game, he, about, was, winning, angry)

→ _____

O6 주어진 말과 동명사를 이용하여 다음 우리말을 영작하시오.

1) 그는 외국에 가는 것을 포기했다. (abroad)

→ _____

2) 내 취미는 음악을 듣는 것이다. (listen to)

→ _____

3) 꿈을 갖지 않는 것은 슬프다. (not)

→ _____

4) 그들은 하이킹 가는 것에 대해 이야기하고 있다. (go hiking)

→ _____

**01** 다음 중 알맞은 것을 고르시오.

1) James decided   reading | to read   the science magazine.

2) I avoided   breaking | to break   my leg.

3) Her sister gave up   losing | to lose   weight.

4) I like   practicing | practice   yoga.

5) They mind   smoking | smoke   in their house.

6) We wish   going | to go   on a trip to Spain.

7) My brother hopes   buying | to buy   a pair of new shoes.

8) The baby started   talking | talks  .

**02** 다음 문장의 틀린 부분에 밑줄을 긋고 바르게 고쳐 쓰시오.

1) Henry enjoys take photos of people.        (→ _____ )

2) They plan do volunteer work              (→ _____ )

3) We finished wash the car.                (→ _____ )

4) Jerry expected solve the puzzle.          (→ _____ )

5) They promised donate some money.         (→ _____ )

**03** 두 문장의 의미가 같도록 빈칸에 알맞은 말을 쓰시오.

1) She hates to catch a cold.

    = She hates _____ a cold.

2) They love swimming in the sea.

    = They love _____ in the sea.

3) He began running an ice cream shop.

    = He began _____ an ice cream shop.

**04** 주어진 말을 이용하여 문장을 완성하시오.

1) He needed a job. He tried _____ a job.  (get)

2) She forgot _____ off the oven so the bread was burnt.  (turn)

3) They are getting fatter so they will stop _____ fried food.  (eat)

4) He remembers _____ with her last night.  (chat)

5) I have the textbook but I forgot _____ it with me.  (bring)

6) Katie saw a nice dress in the show window and she stopped _____ it.  (buy)

O5 다음 문장을 우리말로 해석하시오.

1) He remembered to interview the Olympic medalists.

→ _____

2) He remembered interviewing the Olympic medalists.

→ _____

3) They tried to open the wood gate.

→ _____

4) They tried opening the wood gate.

→ _____

O6 우리말과 일치하도록 주어진 말을 바르게 배열하시오.

1) 그녀는 바이올린 강습을 하기 시작할 것이다. (violin lessons, give, she, begin, to, will)

→ _____

2) 그녀는 뮤지컬 표를 사는 것을 잊어버렸다. (buy, the, she, to, musical, tickets, forgot, for)

→ _____

3) 그는 그녀에게 이메일을 보냈던 것을 잊어버렸다. (her, forgot, an email, he, sending)

→ _____

4) 나는 파리에 한달 동안 머무르리라고 예상한다. (a month, I, expect, Paris, to, in, stay, for)

→ _____

5) 그는 하늘 높이 나는 것을 즐긴다. (flying, he, the sky, enjoys, in, high)

→ _____

6) 그 아기는 우리를 만났던 것을 기억하지 못할 것이다. (meeting, the baby, remember, us, not, will)

→ _____

O7 주어진 말을 이용하여 다음 우리말을 영작하시오.

1) 그는 약을 먹기 위해서 멈추었다. (take some medicine)

→ _____

2) 나는 그 책을 홍보하는 것을 그만두었다. (promote)

→ _____

3) 그들은 학교에 지각하지 않을 것을 약속했다. (late)

→ _____

4) 다이애나(Diana)는 기차로 여행하는 것을 즐긴다. (travel)

→ _____

**01** 다음 중 알맞은 것을 고르시오.

1) Marvin is   playing | played   soccer now.

2) Look at the   singing | sung   boys.

3) He felt   boring | bored .

4) The book is very   boring | bored .

5) My father has   working | worked   there for ten years.

6) Brian is driving a car   making | made   in Korea.

7) She bought a   sleeping | slept   bag yesterday.

8) The game is very   exciting | excited .

9) Many people are   exciting | excited .


**02** 우리말과 일치하도록 빈칸에 알맞은 말을 쓰시오.

1) 나는 충격적인 뉴스를 들었다.

→ I heard the _____ news.

2) 울고 있는 아기는 배가 고파 보인다.

→ The _____ baby looks hungry.

3) 나는 삶은 계란 3개를 샀다.

→ I bought three _____ eggs.

4) 충격 받은 사람들은 조용히 서 있었다.

→ The _____ people stood quietly.

5) 너는 문 앞에 서 있는 남자를 아니?

→ Do you know the man _____ in front of the door?

6) 나는 그녀가 거리를 따라 달려가는 것을 보았다.

→ I saw _____ _____ along the road.


**03** 문장의 밑줄 친 말이 현재분사인지 동명사인지 구분하시오.

1) We went to the swimming pool.          (현재분사, 동명사)

2) The swimming boy is my brother.        (현재분사, 동명사)

3) My friends are skating.                (현재분사, 동명사)

4) My hobby is skating.                   (현재분사, 동명사)

5) Reading books is good for you.         (현재분사, 동명사)

6) The girl reading the book looks happy. (현재분사, 동명사)

---

**04 빈칸에 주어진 단어의 알맞은 형태를 쓰시오.**

1) (surprise)  He was ＿＿＿＿＿＿＿ at the fact.
   This news was ＿＿＿＿＿＿＿.

2) (bore)  I don't like ＿＿＿＿＿＿＿ class.
   The ＿＿＿＿＿＿＿ students are yawning.

3) (tire)  She looks very ＿＿＿＿＿＿＿.
   The work is ＿＿＿＿＿＿＿.

**05 밑줄 친 부분에 유의하여 다음 문장을 우리말로 해석하시오.**

1) My mother is in the waiting room.
   → ＿＿＿＿＿＿＿＿＿＿＿＿＿＿＿＿

2) There is a woman waiting for a bus.
   → ＿＿＿＿＿＿＿＿＿＿＿＿＿＿＿＿

3) She got a gift sent by her father.
   → ＿＿＿＿＿＿＿＿＿＿＿＿＿＿＿＿

4) We watched him riding a bike.
   → ＿＿＿＿＿＿＿＿＿＿＿＿＿＿＿＿

**06 우리말과 일치하도록 주어진 말을 바르게 배열하시오.**

1) 우리는 몇몇 새들이 남쪽으로 날아가는 것을 보았다. (we, birds, flying, saw, some, south)
   → ＿＿＿＿＿＿＿＿＿＿＿＿＿＿＿＿

2) 나는 무대에서 연설하고 있는 사람을 안다. (the, the man, know, a speech, on, making, I, stage)
   → ＿＿＿＿＿＿＿＿＿＿＿＿＿＿＿＿

3) 깨어진 꽃병이 탁자 위에 있었다. (the table, vase, on, was, broken, a)
   → ＿＿＿＿＿＿＿＿＿＿＿＿＿＿＿＿

**07 주어진 말을 이용하여 다음 우리말을 영작하시오.**

1) 우리는 낙엽 위를 걸었다. (fall)
   → ＿＿＿＿＿＿＿＿＿＿＿＿＿＿＿＿

2) 그들은 그녀가 첼로를 연주하는 것을 들었다. (cello)
   → ＿＿＿＿＿＿＿＿＿＿＿＿＿＿＿＿

3) 자고 있는 아기는 행복해 보인다. (sleep)
   → ＿＿＿＿＿＿＿＿＿＿＿＿＿＿＿＿

O1 다음 문장을 분사구문으로 바꿀 때 빈칸에 알맞은 말을 쓰시오.

1) Because she was busy, she could not go there.

→ _____ busy, she could not go there.

2) When he saw me, he said, "Hello."

→ _____, he said, "Hello."

3) Though she had much homework to do, she watched TV all day.

→ _____ to do, she watched TV all day.

4) If you read the book, you can solve the question.

→ _____, you can solve the question.

5) After I washed my hands in the bathroom, I had dinner.

→ _____ in the bathroom, I had dinner.

6) As she doesn't have a car, she has to take a bus.

→ _____, she has to take a bus.

7) If you don't study hard, you will fail the exam.

→ _____, you will fail the exam.


O2 밑줄 친 부분에 유의하여 다음 문장을 우리말로 해석하시오.

1) Loving her, he gives her everything she wants.

→ _____

2) Listening to the music, she is singing a song.

→ _____

3) Having a headache, she continued to take the test.

→ _____

4) Turning to the right, you can find Seoul Station.

→ _____

5) Being at home, he always turns up the volume of the TV.

→ _____

6) Not cooking well, he always eats out.

→ _____

○3 우리말을 영작할 때 틀린 부분에 밑줄을 긋고 비르게 고쳐 쓰시오.

1) 감기에 걸렸기 때문에 나는 집에서 쉬었다.
   → Have a cold, I took a rest at home.          (→ _____ )

2) 나는 유럽에서 공부하는 동안 여러 나라를 방문했다.
   → To study in Europe, I visited several countries.     (→ _____ )

3) 비록 그는 키가 크지는 않지만 훌륭한 농구 선수이다.
   → Don't being tall, he is a great basketball prayer.    (→ _____ )

4) 그녀는 TV를 켜면서 나를 쳐다 보았다.
   → As she turning on TV, she looked at me.        (→ _____ )


○4 우리말과 일치하도록 주어진 말을 바르게 배열하시오.

1) 그를 거리에서 만났을 때 나는 매우 기뻤다.
   (him, was, I, meeting, on, very, the street, pleased)
   → _____

2) 나는 그를 잘 알기 때문에 그에게 돈을 빌려주지 않았다.
   (well, I, didn't, lend, him, him, very, knowing, money)
   → _____

3) 그녀는 팝콘과 콜라를 먹으면서 영화를 보았다.
   (the, and, she, popcorn, watched, eating, coke, movie)
   → _____

4) 그는 부자는 아니지만 늘 행복해한다.
   (not, is, he, being, rich, always, happy)
   → _____


○5 주어진 말과 조건을 이용하여 다음 우리말을 영작하시오.

1) 나의 아버지는 젊었을 때 잘 생기셨었다. (handsome)
   분사구문▶ _____
   부사절▶ When he _____ .

2) 그 아기는 엄마를 찾으면서 울고 있다. (look for)
   분사구문▶ _____
   부사절▶ As _____ .

3) 나는 돈이 없기 때문에 코트를 살 수가 없다. (have)
   분사구문▶ _____
   부사절▶ Because _____ .

**O1** 다음 중 알맞은 것을 고르시오.

1) My father   made ∣ was made   this desk.

2) The pizza   made ∣ was made   by my mom.

3) The police   catch ∣ are caught   thieves.

4) Thieves   catch ∣ are caught   by the police.

5) The hunter   killed ∣ was killed   the poor bird.

6) That skirt   bought ∣ was bought   by me.

7) You will   love ∣ be loved   by everyone.

8) Chinese people   built ∣ was built   the bridge.

**O2** 다음 문장을 수동태로 바꿔 쓰시오.

1) We recycle paper.

→ _____

2) A thief stole the picture.

→ _____

3) Many people will read the book.

→ _____

4) My brother broke Sumi's necklace.

→ _____

5) My nephew collects comic books.

→ _____

**O3** 밑줄 친 부분에 유의하여 다음 문장을 우리말로 해석하시오.

1) A Korean man invented the machine.

→ _____

2) Paper was invented by a Chinese man.

→ _____

3) He found his dog on the street yesterday.

→ _____

4) The cat was found on the street by a girl.

→ _____

○4 다음 문장의 **틀린** 부분에 밑줄을 긋고 바르게 고쳐 쓰시오.

1) Vincent Van Gogh was painted the picture, *Sunflowers*. (→ _____ )

2) The tree will plant by me tomorrow. (→ _____ )

3) The computer is used by my brother last night. (→ _____ )

4) The boxes were moved by he. (→ _____ )

5) These pictures was took in Europe by John a year ago. (→ _____ )

6) Brian was broken the window yesterday. (→ _____ )


○5 우리말과 일치하도록 주어진 말을 바르게 배열하시오.

1) 그 절은 많은 외국인들에 의해 방문을 받는다.

(is, the temple, by, a lot, visited, of, foreigners)

→ _____

2) 그 가난한 소년들은 한 친절한 신사의 도움을 받는다.

(the, helped, poor, are, by, a, kind, boys, gentleman)

→ _____

3) 나의 여행용 가방은 나의 삼촌에 의해 내 방으로 옮겨졌다.

(my, carried, into, was, my room, by, suitcase, my uncle)

→ _____

4) 그 고양이들은 나의 아버지에 의해 키워질 것이다.

(the cats, raised, by, be, will, my father)

→ _____


○6 주어진 말을 이용하여 다음 우리말을 영작하시오.

1) 그 차는 나의 오빠에 의해 수리되었다. (fix)

→ _____

2) 전화기는 벨(Bell)에 의해 발명되었다. (invent)

→ _____

3) 그 일은 토니(Tony)에 의해 끝마쳐질 것이다. (work)

→ _____

4) 너의 옷들은 내일 나에 의해 세탁될 것이다. (clothes)

→ _____

5) 그 영화는 내 친구의 아버지에 의해 만들어졌다. (make)

→ _____

**01** 다음 중 알맞은 것을 고르시오.

1) He   gave ǀ was given   me some water.

2) Some water   gave ǀ was given    for ǀ to   me by him.

3) I   gave ǀ was given   water by him.

4) My grandfather   made ǀ was made   me a kite.

5) The kite   made ǀ was made    for ǀ to   me by my grandfather.

6) The dog   named ǀ was named   Doldol by him.

7) The rules should   follow ǀ be followed   by students.

8) He   lent ǀ was lent   her 10,000 won.

9) Spaghetti   cooked ǀ was cooked   for me by my mom.

10) A present will   send ǀ be sent   to my grandparents by me.

**02** 다음 문장을 수동태로 바꾸어 쓰시오.

1) You should keep your hands warm.

→ _____

2) The song makes us sad.

→ _____

3) We call the girl Sora.

→ _____

4) The teacher teaches students P.E.

→ _____

→ _____

5) She showed us her pictures.

→ _____

→ _____

6) You can do the work.

→ _____

7) My parents brought up the baby in London.

→ _____

8) The children laughed at the poor girl.

→ _____

○3 빈칸에 주어진 단어의 알맞은 형태를 쓰시오.

1) (buy)    A ring _____ for her by him yesterday.

He _____ her a ring yesterday.

2) (give)    We _____ some information by my nephew an hour ago.

My nephew _____ us some information an hour ago.

Some information _____ to us by my nephew an hour ago.

3) (write)    The book may _____ by the famous writer.

The famous writer may _____ the book.

4) (tell)    The boy will _____ the girl the truth.

The truth will _____ to the girl by the boy.

○4 밑줄 친 부분에 유의하여 다음 문장을 우리말로 해석하시오.

1) We must keep the promise.

→ _____

The promise must be kept by us.

→ _____

2) The students asked the teacher a lot of questions.

→ _____

The teacher was asked a lot of questions by the students.

→ _____

3) The members elected him a leader.

→ _____

He was elected a leader by the members.

→ _____

○5 주어진 말을 이용하여 다음 우리말을 영작하시오.

1) 그 식당은 China Factory라고 불린다. (call)

→ _____

2) 그 고아는 누군가에 의해 보살핌을 받아야만 한다. (orphan, take care of)

→ _____

3) 과학은 이 선생님에 의해 학생들에게 가르쳐졌다. (Mr. Lee)

→ _____

4) 그 가방은 유명한 디자이너에 의해 디자인되었을지도 모른다. (may, design)

→ _____

○1 다음 중 알맞은 것을 고르시오.

1) All the money in my house   stole ∣ was stolen  .

2) This tower   built ∣ was built   in 2001.

3) They   speak ∣ are spoken   English and French in Canada.

4) Japanese   speaks ∣ is spoken   in Japan.

5) We   know ∣ are known   the movie star very well.

6) Many soldiers   killed ∣ were killed   in the Vietnam War.

7) The World Cup will   hold ∣ be held   in a year.


○2 우리말과 일치하도록 빈칸에 알맞은 말을 쓰시오.

1) 이 교복은 학생들을 위해서 디자인되었다.
→ This school uniform _____ _____ for students.

2) 보름달은 추석에 볼 수 있다.
→ A full moon can _____ _____ at Chuseok.

3) 너희들은 용서를 받을 것이다.
→ You will _____ _____.

4) 그 영화는 많은 사람들에게 알려졌다.
→ The movie is _____ _____ many people.

5) 그 책상은 먼지로 덮여있다.
→ The desk is _____ _____ dust.

6) 나의 여동생이 곧 태어날 것이다.
→ My younger sister _____ _____ _____ soon.

7) 그녀의 부모님은 그녀의 시험 결과에 기뻐했다.
→ Her parents were _____ _____ her exam result.


○3 빈칸에 알맞은 전치사를 쓰시오.

1) My sister is interested _____ playing the guitar.

2) The box is filled _____ chocolate.

3) This chair was put here _____ someone.

4) My teacher was satisfied _____ my answer.

5) They were surprised _____ the news.

6) The table was made _____ my father.

○4 〈by + 목적격〉이 생략 가능한 것에 괄호를 치고 전체 문장을 해석하시오.

1) German is spoken in Germany and Austria by people.

→ _____

2) The student was punished by his father.

→ _____

3) America was discovered by Columbus.

→ _____

4) These shoes are produced in this company by them.

→ _____

5) My house was broken into by someone.

→ _____

○5 우리말과 일치하도록 주어진 말을 바르게 배열하시오.

1) 이 바위는 이틀 전에 여기로 옮겨졌다. (this, moved, two, rock, was, days, here, ago)

→ _____

2) 너의 책은 전 세계에서 읽혀질 것이다. (your, read, all, be, over, will, book, the world)

→ _____

3) 그 섬은 꽃과 나무들로 덮여있었다. (was, with, the island, flowers, covered, and, trees)

→ _____

4) 이 여배우는 아시아에 있는 모든 사람들에게 알려져 있다.

(is, in, known, actress, this, everyone, to, Asia)

→ _____

○6 주어진 말을 이용하여 다음 우리말을 영작하시오.

1) 인터넷은 매일 사용된다. (the Internet)

→ _____

2) 그는 영화에 관심이 있다. (interest)

→ _____

3) 이 대학은 1960년에 설립되었다. (university, found)

→ _____

4) 이 서랍은 편지로 가득 차 있다. (drawer)

→ _____

## 01 다음 중 알맞은 것을 고르시오.

1) Kate will write a book review  before | after  she reads the book.

2) He will look after the dog  until | after  it dies.

3) We will take a picture  before | that  we get in the car.

4) He smiled at her  as | though  she saw him.

5)  Though | While  my sister was in Paris, she studied fashion design.

6) When she  will watch | watches  the movie, she will cry.

## 02 우리말과 일치하도록 빈칸에 알맞은 말을 보기에서 골라 쓰시오.

| 보기 | after | before | until | when | while |

1) 해가 질 때까지 우리는 해변에 있었다.

→ We were on the beach _____ the sunset.

2) 그가 운전하는 동안 우리는 차 안에서 잤다.

→ _____ he was driving, we slept in the car.

3) 나는 그를 처음 만났을 때 좋아하지 않았다.

→ I didn't like him _____ I first met him.

4) 방학이 시작하기 전에 나는 선생님에게 상담을 받으러 갔다.

→ I went to my teacher for advice _____ the vacation started.

5) 우리는 수업 후에 간식을 먹을 것이다.

→ We will have snacks _____ class.

## 03 다음 문장을 우리말로 해석하시오.

1) We will talk to each other until the bus comes.

→ _____

2) As Susan sat on the chair, it broke.

→ _____

3) They will do the dishes after they have lunch.

→ _____

4) He will have a cup of coffee before he attends the meeting.

→ _____

04 우리말과 일치하도록 주어진 말을 바르게 배열하시오.

1) 그가 퇴원할 때까지 그녀는 그를 돌볼 것이다.

(him, until, she, the, hospital, take care of, leaves, will, he)

→ _____

7) 나는 그 소식을 들었을 때 아무 말도 할 수 없었다.

(the, I, when, anything, couldn't, I, heard, news, say)

→ _____

3) 우리는 저녁을 먹기 전에 농구를 할 것이다.

(will, before, basketball, we, dinner, have, play, we)

→ _____

4) 그들은 방을 청소하는 동안 창문을 열었다.

(opened, cleaning, the, window, they, while, were, the, room, they)

→ _____

5) 그녀가 가게에 들어왔을 때 그가 나갔다.

(as, into, went, she, the, store, came, he, out)

→ _____

6) 그들이 우승자를 발표한 후에 우리는 집에 갈 것이다.

(announce, we, after, go, the, winner, will, home, they)

→ _____


05 주어진 말을 이용하여 다음 우리말을 영작하시오.

1) 그들은 책을 폈을 때 편지를 발견했다. (as)

→ _____

2) 나는 엄마가 집에 올 때까지 기다릴 것이다. (come home)

→ _____

3) 그는 빨래를 한 후에 쉴 것이다. (do the laundry)

→ _____

4) 그녀는 요리하기 전에 재료를 살 것이다. (ingredients)

→ _____

5) 우리는 산책하는 동안 무지개를 보았다. (take a walk)

→ _____

6) 그는 아기였을 때 자주 웃었다. (smile)

→ _____

**01** 다음 중 알맞은 것을 고르시오.

1) He stayed in bed   because | because of   his sickness.

2) Ann wants to be a relay-runner   because | because of   she runs fast.

3) We were hungry,   as | so   we ate a lot at the buffet restaurant.

4) It was so light that the little boy   could | couldn't   lift it.

5) The tea is so hot that I   can | can't   drink it.

**02** 우리말과 일치하도록 빈칸에 알맞은 말을 쓰시오.

1) 나는 독서를 좋아하기 때문에 매달 여러 권의 책을 산다.

→ _____ I like reading, I buy several books each month.

2) 학생들은 태풍 때문에 학교에 가지 않았다.

→ The students didn't go to school _____ _____ the typhoon.

3) 그는 너무 수줍어서 그녀에게 말을 건넬 수 없었다.

→ He was _____ shy _____ he _____ talk to her.

4) 그들은 게을러서 아무것도 하지 않았다.

→ They were lazy, _____ they did nothing.

**03** 두 문장의 뜻이 같도록 빈칸에 알맞은 말을 쓰시오.

1) They are clever enough to answer any questions.

= They are _____ _____ _____ _____ _____ answer any questions.

2) He was too nervous to say a word.

= He was _____ _____ _____ _____ _____ say a word.

3) She ate too much, so she had a stomachache.

= _____ _____ _____ _____ _____, she had a stomachache.

○4 다음 두 문장을 한 문장으로 나타낼 때 빈칸에 알맞은 접속사를 쓰시오.

1) I wanted to play with my friends. So I called my friends.

→ I called my friends _____ I wanted to play with them.

2) The traffic was very heavy. The cars couldn't move.

→ The traffic was _____ _____ _____ the cars couldn't move.

3) They didn't play football because it was raining heavily.

→ They didn't play football _____ _____ the heavy rain.

4) Harry slept all day because he was very tired.

→ Harry was very tired _____ he slept all day.


○5 우리말과 일치하도록 주어진 말을 바르게 배열하시오.

1) 우리는 너무 시끄러워서 잘 수 없었다.

(noisy, it, sleep, that, was, couldn't, so, we)

→ _____

2) 그는 그 도둑을 잡을 정도로 용감했다.

(enough, catch, brave, he, to, was, the, thief)

→ _____

3) 그녀는 장난감 때문에 여동생과 싸웠다.

(she, her, sister, because, fought, of, the, toy, with)

→ _____

4) 딸기가 맛있어서 우리는 더 먹었다.

(ate, so, the, strawberries, we, were, more, delicious)

→ _____


○6 우리말과 일치하도록 빈칸에 알맞은 말을 쓰시오.

1) 그 소녀는 너무 약해서 등산을 할 수 없다.

→ _____ to climb a mountain.

2) 그들은 경기에 이길 정도로 강하다.

→ _____ to win the game.

3) 셔츠가 너무 더러워서 그녀는 그것을 입을 수 없었다.

→ The shirt was so _____ .

**01** 다음 중 알맞은 것을 고르시오.

1) If | Unless   they are tall, they can't be basketball players.

2) If | Though   Kate answers the question, she will pass the test.

3) I will eat it   that | if   you don't eat the cookie.

4) She knows   though | that   he is a spy.

5) That | Though   he was sick, he couldn't go to see a doctor.

6) If she   will go | goes   to Paris, she will visit the Louvre Museum.

**02** 우리말과 일치하도록 빈칸에 알맞은 접속사를 쓰시오.

1) 나는 그가 어리석다고 생각한다.

→ I think _____ he is foolish.

2) 비록 우리가 자주 만나지 못할지라도 우리는 전화로 매일 이야기한다.

→ _____ we don't meet often, we talk on the phone every day.

3) 케빈이 실수를 하지 않는다면 만점을 받을 것이다.

→ _____ Kevin makes a mistake, he will get a perfect score.

4) 내가 그 소설가를 만난다면 사인을 받을 것이다.

→ _____ I meet the novelist, I will get his autograph.

5) 나는 그가 나를 기억하는지 궁금하다.

→ I wonder _____ he remembers me.

6) 그가 자전거를 타지 못한다면, 자전거여행을 가지 못할 것이다.

→ He can't go on a bicycle trip _____ he rides a bike.

7) 그들이 휴가를 얻는다면 그들은 여행할 것이다.

→ They will travel _____ they get a vacation.

**03** 두 문장의 뜻이 같도록 문장을 완성하시오.

1) You will regret it unless you listen to me.

= You will regret it if _____.

2) I want to know if he will go to the baseball stadium.

= I want to know _____.

○4 다음 문장을 우리말로 해석하시오.

1) If it is hot tomorrow, we will go to the water park.

→ _____

2) Unless Suzie is healthy, she will catch a cold.

→ _____

3) Though he was hurt, he saved others.

→ _____

4) She believes that they invented a time machine.

→ _____

○5 우리말과 일치하도록 주어진 말을 바르게 배열하시오.

1) 나는 돈을 좀 모은다면 유럽여행을 갈 것이다.

(travel, some, money, if, will, save, I, Europe, I, to)

→ _____

2) 그는 영화 표가 없다면 영화를 볼 수 없다.

(a movie ticket, can't, unless, see, has, he, the movie, he)

→ _____

3) 그녀는 그가 영웅이라고 생각한다.

(thinks, he, a hero, she, that, is)

→ _____

4) 비록 그들이 외국인일지라도 한국어를 잘 말한다.

(foreigners, speak, though, are, they, Korean, they, very well )

→ _____

5) 그들이 우유를 마시지 않는다면 사지 않을 것이다.

(don't, if, drink, they, it, milk, they, buy, won't)

→ _____

○6 주어진 말을 이용하여 다음 우리말을 영작하시오.

1) 그들이 학생이 아니라면 그들은 할인을 받을 수 없다.  (unless, get a discount)

→ _____

2) 에이미(Amy)가 정직하다면 거짓말하지 않을 것이다.  (honest)

→ _____

3) 비록 그는 유명하지만 인기가 있지는 않다.  (though)

→ _____

**01 밑줄 친 부분을 바르게 고쳐 쓰시오.**

1) Close the window, <u>but</u> you might catch a cold.  (→ _____ )
2) Turn on the light, <u>or</u> you can see it well.  (→ _____ )
3) They will eat either pizza <u>and</u> fried chicken.  (→ _____ )
4) Kevin likes not only English <u>and</u> also mathematics.  (→ _____ )
5) Neither he <u>or</u> she is my friend.  (→ _____ )
6) He <u>so</u> well as she is a student.  (→ _____ )
7) This is <u>not</u> a history book but also a comic book.  (→ _____ )

**02 우리말과 일치하도록 빈칸에 알맞은 접속사를 쓰시오.**

1) 그뿐만 아니라 나도 시험에 통과했다.
→ _____ he _____ I passed the test.

2) 그녀가 아니라 그가 내 사촌이다.
→ _____ she _____ he is my cousin.

3) 그와 그녀 둘 다 그 영화를 봤다.
→ _____ he _____ she saw the movie.

4) 나뿐만 아니라 그도 작년에 제주도에 갔었다.
→ He _____ _____ _____ I went to Jejudo last year.

5) 그녀나 그가 그 강아지를 돌볼 것이다.
→ _____ she _____ he will take care of the puppy.

6) 그들도 우리도 애완동물이 없다.
→ _____ they _____ we have a pet.

**03 빈칸에 알맞은 be동사의 현재시제로 바꾸어 쓰시오.**

1) Both Kate and I _____ tall.
2) Either Harry or you _____ class president.
3) Not only Paul but also I _____ busy.
4) Not I but he _____ her friend.
5) She as well as I _____ pretty.

04 두 문장의 뜻이 같도록 빈칸에 알맞은 말을 쓰시오.

1) Not only Susan but also I like reading.

= I _____ _____ _____ Susan like reading.

2) Unless you speak loudly, they can't hear you.

= Speak loudly, _____ they can't hear you.

3) If you practice hard, you will win the contest.

= Practice hard, _____ you will win the contest.

4) If you don't leave now, you will be late for school.

= Leave now, _____ you will be late for school.

05 다음 두 문장을 한 문장으로 나타낼 때 빈칸에 알맞은 접속사를 쓰시오.

1) He ate a sandwich. He ate an apple, too.

→ He ate _____ a sandwich _____ an apple.

2) I don't know him. I don't know her, either.

→ I know _____ him _____ her.

3) She can speak English fluently. Or she can speak Chinese fluently.

→ She can speak _____ English _____ Chinese fluently.

06 우리말과 일치하도록 주어진 말을 바르게 배열하시오.

1) 영화클럽에 가입해라, 그러면 너는 많은 영화를 볼 수 있다.

(and, movies, join, you, a lot of, can, the movie club, see)

→ _____

2) 샌드위치를 먹어라, 그렇지 않으면 너는 나중에 배고플 것이다.

(hungry, will, the sandwich, be, or, you, later, eat)

→ _____

3) 그도 그녀도 역사박물관에 가지 않았다.

(went, neither, the history museum, he, she, to, nor)

→ _____

4) 그는 과학뿐만 아니라 수학도 좋아한다.

(mathematics, well, he, as, science, as, likes)

→ _____

5) 그가 아니라 그녀가 내 담임선생님이다.

(not, homeroom teacher, he, my, but, is, she)

→ _____

**01** 다음 중 알맞은 것을 고르시오.

1) I thought that he   is | was   happy.

2) He hoped that she   will | would   come back soon.

3) He thought that she   has wanted | wanted   the bag.

4) Dad said that time   flies | flew   like an arrow.

5) My brother learned that water   boils | boiled   at 100 ℃.

6) We knew that the Vietnam War   had ended | ended   in 1975.

7) They know that he   arrived | had arrived   in Seoul last weekend.

8) Mary thinks that I   have been | had been   to Paris before.

9) I heard that he   was working | is working   for a bank then.

10) I know that she   had lived | has lived   in Ilsan since 1999.

**02** 주절의 시제를 과거형으로 바꿀 때 빈칸에 알맞은 말을 쓰시오.

1) I know that she has a nice car.

→ I knew that she _____ a nice car.

2) She thinks that he can ski.

→ She thought that he _____ ski.

3) They believe that Brian has lost his cat.

→ They believed that Brian _____ _____ his cat.

4) He knows that Columbus discovered America in 1492.

→ He knew that Columbus _____ America in 1492.

5) She hopes that they will succeed.

→ She hoped that they _____ _____.

6) He thinks that she is going to call him.

→ He thought that she _____ going to call him.

7) My mother says that the early bird catches the worm.

→ My mother said that the early bird _____ the worm.

8) They believe that he and she are kind.

→ They believed that he and she _____ kind.

○3 밑줄 친 부분을 바르게 고쳐 쓰시오.

1) He said that he will finish reading the book. (→ _____ )

2) My teacher said that Japan had attacked the American Navy in 1940. (→ _____ )

3) I think that he was at home since yesterday. (→ _____ )

4) My father always told me that a friend in need was a friend indeed. (→ _____ )

5) He knew that France was in Europe. (→ _____ )

○4 우리말과 일치하도록 주어진 말을 바르게 배열하시오.

1) 우리는 많은 외국인이 한국을 매년 방문한다고 생각한다.
(we, foreigners, that, a lot of, think, Korea, every, visit, year)
→ _____

2) 그녀는 그녀의 여동생이 열심히 공부하기를 바랐다.
(study, that, her, hoped, would, she, sister, hard)
→ _____

3) 우리는 지구가 태양의 주위를 돈다고 배웠다.
(we, goes, learned, that, around ,the Earth, the Sun)
→ _____

4) 그는 매일 1시에 점심을 먹는다고 나에게 말했다.
(o'clock, told he, at, one, has, lunch, he, me, that, every day)
→ _____

○5 주어진 말을 이용하여 다음 우리말을 영작하시오.

1) 에디슨(Edison)이 전구를 발명했다고 내 친구가 말했다. (the light bulb)
→ _____

2) 나는 그녀가 예쁘다고 생각했다. (pretty)
→ _____

3) 우리는 그녀가 곧 돌아올 거라고 믿었다. (come back)
→ _____

4) 나의 어머니는 연습은 완벽을 만든다고 말했다. (practice, perfect)
→ _____

**01** 평서문의 직접화법을 간접화법으로 바꾸어 쓰시오.

1) He often says, "I will be a dentist."

→ _____

2) He said, "I will learn how to drive."

→ _____

3) She said to me, "I want to visit you."

→ _____

4) My teacher said to me, "You have to study harder."

→ _____

5) The man said to her, "I am waiting for you."

→ _____

6) She said to the man, "You can park your car."

→ _____

**02** 의문문의 직접화법을 간접화법으로 바꾸어 쓰시오.

1) My father said to me, "Where is your mother?"

→ _____

2) The woman said to him, "Why are you crying?"

→ _____

3) She said to me, "How do you go to school?"

→ _____

4) I said to him, "What time do you have breakfast?"

→ _____

5) His teacher said to them, "Are you doing your homework?

→ _____

6) The teacher said to the girl, "Can you read the sentence?"

→ _____

7) I said to Sumi, "Do you have a computer?"

→ _____

**03** 간접화법을 직접화법으로, 직접화법을 간접화법으로 바꿀 때 **틀린** 부분에 밑줄을 긋고 바르게 고쳐 쓰시오.

1) He said, "I will go to London."

　→ He told that he would go to London.　　　　　　(→ ＿＿＿＿＿＿＿＿ )

2) He said to me, "What is your favorite food?"

　→ He told me what my favorite food was.　　　　　( ˙ ＿＿＿＿＿＿＿＿ )

3) The waiter said to me, "Are you ready to order?"

　→ The waiter asked me that I was ready to order.　(→ ＿＿＿＿＿＿＿＿ )

4) Mary said to him, "How did you go to Jejudo?"

　→ Mary asked him how did he go to Jejudo.　　　(→ ＿＿＿＿＿＿＿＿ )

5) My brother told me that I looked pretty.

　→ My brother said to me, "I look pretty."　　　　(→ ＿＿＿＿＿＿＿＿ )

6) She asked him how old he was.

　→ She said to him, "How old I am?"　　　　　　(→ ＿＿＿＿＿＿＿＿ )

**04** 우리말과 일치하도록 주어진 말을 바르게 배열하시오.

1) 그녀는 그 사실을 믿을 수 없다고 말했다.

　(she, not, believe, said, that, she, could, the fact)

　→ ＿＿＿＿＿＿＿＿＿＿＿＿＿＿＿＿＿＿＿＿＿＿＿＿＿

2) 그는 그의 어머니에게 스페인어를 배우고 싶다고 말했다.

　(learn, his mother, told, to, that, he, he, wanted, Spanish)

　→ ＿＿＿＿＿＿＿＿＿＿＿＿＿＿＿＿＿＿＿＿＿＿＿＿＿

3) 그녀는 나에게 얼마나 자주 나의 고향을 방문하는지 물어보았다.

　(me, visited, asked, she, my, how often, I, hometown)

　→ ＿＿＿＿＿＿＿＿＿＿＿＿＿＿＿＿＿＿＿＿＿＿＿＿＿

**05** 다음 우리말을 영작하시오.

1) 그는 야구를 좋아한다고 나에게 말했다.

　→ ＿＿＿＿＿＿＿＿＿＿＿＿＿＿＿＿＿＿＿＿＿＿＿＿＿

2) 그녀는 나에게 내가 어디에 사는지 물어보았다.

　→ ＿＿＿＿＿＿＿＿＿＿＿＿＿＿＿＿＿＿＿＿＿＿＿＿＿

3) 그는 나에게 스키를 탈 수 있는지 물어보았다.

　→ ＿＿＿＿＿＿＿＿＿＿＿＿＿＿＿＿＿＿＿＿＿＿＿＿＿

**01** 밑줄 친 부분을 바르게 고쳐 쓰시오.

1) If it was cold, we will not go hiking.   (→ _____ )

2) If Susan studies harder, she would pass the test.   (→ _____ )

3) If I was you, I would help them.   (→ _____ )

4) If he had more money, he will buy snacks.   (→ _____ )

5) If I became a writer, I will write a history novel.   (→ _____ )

6) If they were brave, they will go hang gliding.   (→ _____ )

**02** 빈칸에 주어진 단어의 알맞은 형태를 쓰시오.

1) If the rumor _____ true, people would be surprised.  (be)

2) If it _____ too far from here, we will not go there.  (be)

3) If we invited her to the party, she _____.  (come)

4) If I bake bread, I _____ it with my friends.  (eat)

5) If Kate _____ enough time, she would go on a trip.  (have)

6) If he _____ a house, it will be a two story house.  (build)

**03** 두 문장의 뜻이 같도록 빈칸에 알맞은 말을 쓰시오.

1) As we are not adults, we cannot vote.

= If we _____ adults, we _____ _____.

2) As she doesn't remember the password, she can't log in.

= If she _____ the password, she _____ _____ in.

3) As the car is expensive, we can't buy it.

= If the car _____ _____ expensive, we _____
_____ it.

4) If they did their best, they could have better results.

= As they _____ _____ their best, they _____
_____ better results.

5) If he had more time, he could play with his friend.

= As he _____ _____ more time, he _____
_____ with his friend.

04 다음 문장을 우리말로 해석하시오.

1) If I am sick, she will take care of me.

→ _____

2) If she spoke English, she would go to Canada.

→ _____

3) If Amy takes pictures, she will upload them on the Internet.

→ _____

4) If we were in the same class, we could study together.

→ _____


05 우리말과 일치하도록 주어진 말을 바르게 배열하시오.

1) 그들이 귀신을 본다면 소리를 지를 것이다.

(scream, see, they, a ghost, if, will, they)

→ _____

2) 내가 텔레비전에 나온다면 정말 좋을 텐데.

(on, I, really, appeared, be, TV, I, happy, would, if)

→ _____

3) 우리가 사과나무를 심는다면 사과를 먹을 수 있을 것이다.

(eat, if, apples, plant, we, apple, can, trees, we)

→ _____

4) 휴대전화가 있다면 친구에게 전화를 할 텐데.

(I, my, if, I, friend, had, would, a cell phone, call)

→ _____

5) 그가 제주도에 간다면 한라산에 오를 것이다.

(he, Jejudo, if, goes, climb, to, he, will, Mt. Halla)

→ _____


06 다음 우리말을 영작하시오.

1) 나는 배고프면 요리를 할 것이다.

→ _____

2) 케빈이 여기에 온다면 우리와 같이 여행을 할 수 있을 텐데.

→ _____

**O1** 빈칸에 주어진 단어의 알맞은 형태를 쓰시오.

1) If Suzie _____ his book, she would have given it to him.  (find)

2) If you heard the song, you _____ it.  (love)

3) If he _____ his key, he could have opened the drawer.  (not, lose)

4) If a miracle _____, we would be surprised.  (happen)

5) If they _____ the secret, no one would have known it.  (keep)

6) If she hadn't left home, she _____ comfortably.  (live)

**O2** 우리말과 일치하도록 주어진 말을 이용하여 빈칸을 채우시오.

1) 그들이 그를 인터뷰했다면 그를 고용했을 텐데.  (interview, hire)

→ If they _____ him, they _____ him.

2) 그가 그 그림을 샀다면 많은 돈을 벌었을 텐데.  (buy, make)

→ If he _____ the painting, he _____ a lot of money.

3) 우리가 그것을 증명한다면 우리는 유명해질 텐데.  (prove, become)

→ If we _____ it, we _____ famous.

4) 소방대원이 그를 구해주지 않았다면 그는 죽었을 텐데.  (rescue, die)

→ If the firefighter _____ him, he _____.

5) 우리가 음식을 남겨놨더라면 그들이 먹을 수 있었을 텐데.  (leave, eat)

→ If we _____ some food, they _____ it.

**O3** 두 문장의 뜻이 같도록 빈칸에 알맞은 말을 쓰시오.

1) As we didn't watch the drama, we couldn't know the story.

= If we _____ _____ the drama, we _____
_____ _____ the story.

2) If she hadn't called me, I couldn't have recognized her.

= As she _____ me, I _____ her.

3) As she didn't forgive him, he couldn't meet her.

= If she _____ _____ him, he _____
_____ _____ her.

O4 다음 문장을 우리말로 해석하시오.

1) If Susan hadn't lost her sunglasses, she could have worn them.

→ _____

2) If they had met him, they would have respected him.

→ _____

3) If he rode a bike, he wouldn't walk to school.

→ _____

4) If we had gone to bed earlier, we wouldn't have been sleepy.

→ _____

O5 우리말과 일치하도록 주어진 말을 바르게 배열하시오.

1) 우리가 그 영어선생님을 좋아했더라면 영어를 더 열심히 공부했을 텐데.

(liked, if, studied, the English teacher, had, we, would, English, have, harder, we)

→ _____

2) 그가 법을 어겼더라면 후회했을 텐데.

(broken, if, had, have, it, he, the, law, regretted, would, he)

→ _____

3) 그들이 우리를 돕지 않았더라면 우리는 이것을 끝낼 수 없었을 텐데.

(they, if, helped, couldn't, us, hadn't, finished, it, we, have)

→ _____

4) 그녀가 인기가 있지 않았더라면 바쁘지 않았을 텐데.

(hadn't, if, she, have, popular, been, couldn't, busy, she, been)

→ _____

5) 그가 비행기를 가지고 있다면 어디든지 날아갈 텐데.

(he, if, had, would, he, everywhere, a plane, fly)

→ _____

O6 다음 우리말을 영작하시오.

1) 그가 공부를 열심히 했더라면 의사가 되었을 텐데.

→ _____

2) 그녀가 천사라면 날개가 있을 텐데.

→ _____

# Memo